For my father.

INTRODUCTION

Originally, I wanted to be a Jungian. We can parse what I mean by "originally" in a minute but given the audience I am hoping to reach let's start with Jung instead with whom some of you may be unfamiliar. Carl Gustav Jung was the rebellious, flawed, brilliant psychologist who if he did not invent the idea that suprapersonal archetypal forces are intensely influential on the course of our lives, certainly codified it in a way that makes it impossible to turn to any other source in seeking to understand its origins. There's that word "origin" again, not for the last time, and indeed that is a big part of what you will find discussed within this book. Perhaps you are even confused why the focus is on a word everyone knows when I am also throwing around words like "suprapersonal" (which my spellchecker doesn't even recognize). The intent with this book is to reach out to fans of the true crime genre, which is wildly popular, and to make it both accessible to a popular audience but challenging as well. If a word pops up here and there you don't immediately recognize I trust you have a handy AI nearby who will help you with that. At some point in puberty, I made the misguided decision that my virginity would be ended more quickly if I learned to throw around the occasional five-dollar word. I was a pretentious kid. Of course, it didn't work nearly as well as I hoped, but I couldn't play guitar and I was terrible at sports so I worked with what I had. Later in life I realized that learning how to cook was much more effective, and even that paled in comparison to being an end-of-life caregiver which saw me hanging out with a lot of nurses. Now, single in my 50's, it seems likely I will never have sex again, which I am surprisingly sanguine about. "Sanguine" is also an interesting word. One the one hand it means to be cheerful and optimistic. It also means bloody.

Humans have a negativity bias for very good reasons. Our ancestors who spent more time marveling over wildflowers than worrying about what might be hiding among them got eaten. That bias is so strong we have turned it into entertainment. Even the gentlest movies and books contain some level of conflict or there would be little drama to care about. Personally, I rarely need much help being negative and I've even got a touch of a squeamish streak. One of my favorite shows is *The Walking Dead,* even though I cried like a little girl when Carl died and tend to avert my gaze from the screen when something really gross happens. One time in culinary school a recipe required us to peel the skin from chickens by tugging it off. I wound up throwing up and didn't have any easy time living it down. Interestingly, it was much less of an issue when I was taking care of the dying. It's much easier to like people when they're dying, or at least forgive them. Which brings us to murder, to what I am sure is your great relief, the chief subject of this book. True crime podcasts, books and documentaries proliferate well beyond their fictional counterparts, themselves innumerable. Nothing is more negative than malevolence, and some of the details you will find in this book are not for the faint of heart. Although some cases involve psychopaths, that subject deserves its own book. Of note though is how little agreement on what psychopathy actually is. Forensic psychology, and really psychology in general, is a troubled field (again, likely the subject of its own book). Far from its depiction in popular entertainment, forensic psychology is only rarely used for profiling *unknown* suspects and often enough is utterly useless to their identification. That doesn't mean *Hannibal* isn't one of my favorite shows of all time and given that Dr. Lecter and I are both great cooks and excellent dressers we have much in common. We simply have almost never caught anyone simply as a result of a psychological profile. As we will see in the case of Richard Ramirez, the so-called Night Stalker who terrorized Los Angeles in the 1980's, even with a very good description, a unique shoeprint and the use of rarified ammunition, he was extraordinarily difficult to catch. The almost simple-minded psychological attempt to catch him on the belief that he would return to a dentist because of severe tooth pain was seen as a waste of money, which resulted in a lost opportunity and the death of at least four more people. Forensic psychology is very much the red-headed stepchild of the larger discipline of criminology. Police have absolutely no interest in whether or not an unknown assailant wasn't hugged enough by his father, they just want to know something that will help them catch him. In your average television show a crack psychologist, all but worshipped for their quirky genius by their colleagues, notices some detail in a crime scene in the first five minutes of the show. Before ten minutes are up they have a spot on description of the killer. By the half hour mark they're on his tail and have caught him, within five minutes he proudly confesses, sealing the deal. At the forty two minute mark we see the whole team cheerfully enjoying a beer together before returning home to their stable marriages where they apologize to their wife for how busy they've been for the past week catching this terrible killer. The next week they do the same thing all over again. This not at all how real investigations work and it is even less how forensic psychology works. Most murders are utterly banal. My favorite example is man who emptied his gun in his roommates directions after he ate the last Hot Pocket. For the who don't know, a Hot Pocket is a delicious frozen snack. I love them, but I could hardly imagine killing someone over them. Luckily the man was a very poor shot, hitting his roommate only once in the ass, a wound he survived. The real potential of forensic psychology is the early identification and intervention with young people who *might* grow up to be what are known as "life course persistent offenders". However, the United States has a horrible record when it comes to supporting and protecting children. Sometimes our culture is as callous and unemotional as any serial killer.

Compared to our peers in the developed institutional West, the United States is an absolute basket case. We are the richest and most powerful by far, we also have the worst rate of childhood poverty, the worst access to medical care particularly mental health care, the worst food insecurity, the worst housing insecurity, the shortest life expectancy and the worst economic inequality. Arguably as a direct result of that we have the highest rate of suicide, rape and murder. Our murder rate is ten times the rate of that in our closest peers. Because certain elements of our legislature, not exclusively right of center but damn close, are so paranoid that any accomplishment by the government will have a halo effect which will contradict the hundreds of billions of dollars that have been spent to convince the public that our government is entirely incompetent and evil we can't seem to build so much as a bridge in this country anymore. Grover Norquist built an entire career around the one pithy phrase that the US government should be "small enough to be drowned in a bathtub." If it was some punk like Kim Jon Il would come along and do just that. So we do have big spending on the military, which is $30 billion dollars more than the spending of the next ten countries *combined.* A recent study concluded that every individual murder costs somewhere between $15-$25 million *each.* We are already spending quite a lot of money to respond to crime, and very little on simple programs that would likely prevent much of it. It is impossible to stop it all. Any human system of sufficient scale will always include injustice as a nonzero phenomenon. Forensic psychology may not do much to catch murderers before they strike, but it is doing quite a bit to help us understand them, which provides us an opportunity to prevent them from becoming killers in the first place. It is an opportunity we seem determined to waste.

As I mentioned, forensic psychology is a troubled science, in part because the studies involved in large part focus on criminals. They are quite interesting of course, but they are hardly the only people who interact with the law. To some degree or other, we all interact with the law whether we realize it or not. Criminals, and prisoners in particular, aren't merely interesting but also easily motivated. Put a little money in their commissary account, or tempt them with a trip off of the prison grounds to get a brain scan or some such, and they will clamor for the chance. Now try and do a study on prosecutorial misconduct, a pressing issue in my opinion, and I would be surprised if you could get any cooperation at all. Or a different one on what motivates legislators to put a little pork in some omnibus bill. Or one about the experience of police who have killed someone in the line of duty. All of these things technically fall under the umbrella of forensic psychology, but none of them are studied. Even within the criminal sphere you are much more likely to get noticed for a study about serial killers than for one about shoplifting. The blind spot involved is huge, and we don't know what we are missing as a result. Don't worry, although I veer a bit from the standard path in this book, there is no essay on shoplifting (although I do mention graffiti artists briefly). Nonetheless, I do think it is important for people to get a better understanding of forensic psychology than your favorite TV show is going to offer, and if talking about murder gets your attention that works for me too. Obviously, I did not pursue a master's degree only to then focus on people kiting checks.

Overall I think what studying crime reveals is that it is intensely related to issues of *identity*. For now, that is as much a conjecture as anything, though I am working to gather enough data to escalate it to a testable hypothesis and maybe get it to the point where it could be called a theory. A lot of people misunderstand all three of those words, and think a theory isn't really a solid idea. Einstein's theory of relativity has been proven true over and over again, and the internet you are probably using to read this right now wouldn't be possible without taking it into account. Though again I encourage you to google anything unfamiliar a conjecture is an attempt to explain something without any evidence to support it, a hypothesis has more evidence attached but is still a bit of a guess and when an hypothesis grows up it becomes a theory and stays a theory even after reams of empirical information support it because science always allows that a better explanation could come along at any minute. For now, the preliminary evidence as I have seen it shows that particularly those who have been traumatized in some way are much more likely to commit murder, and trauma tends to make us question our identity. As a result, over and over again, there are examples of murderers who kill either to defend their identity against something, or to assert their identity to the world. It is a very powerful force capable of motivating anyone to do anything. In some cases, terrible things.

THE TERRORIST WHO WASN'T

Near closing time at 2:00 AM on June 12, 2016 Omar Mateen walked up to the Pulse Nightclub in Orlando, Florida and immediately opened fire at the entrance using a semiautomatic rifle as well as a semiautomatic pistol he had legally purchased in the week before the attack. A security guard attempted to engage him but withdrew in the face of superior firepower. The guard, Adam Gruler, an off-duty Orlando police officer, within minutes called in a police response that quickly grew to epic proportions. Meanwhile, Mateen began his first of several calls to 911, claiming the attack was revenge against US military strikes overseas and that more attacks like his would be happening soon. Further, he told terrified patrons he was going to force them wear suicide bomb vests and send them out to kill police. During a call with hostage negotiators Mateen claimed there was a car bomb outside and that additionally he was wearing a suicide vest. Three hours later, using a combination of controlled detonations and impacting the building with an armored vehicle, a breach in the wall was formed which allowed hostages to escape and SWAT to infiltrate. Mateen was killed after engaging a dozen officers in a gun battle.

Omar Mateen had shown behavioral problems since grade school causing him to be put into a special class. School officials claimed his parents enabled his behavior. Mateen attacked the Pulse Nightclub with legally purchased weapons, committing what was the worst mass shooting up to that point, and remains the deadliest act against the LGBTQ+ community. Despite making many claims of his connections to Islamic terrorism before and during the shooting, his claims seem at best specious and possibly even indicative of delusional tendencies. Mateen may have been conflicted about his own sexuality. He may have used steroids which can be positively associated with high-risk sexual behavior and aggression. Terrorism cannot be entirely discounted as Mateen was undergoing a self-radicalization process and had known associates who committed terrorist acts.

Terrorist organizations strongly encourage "lone wolf" acts. Mateen's life path and criminal act are more consistent with the still poorly defined profile of mass shootings than politically motivated acts of terrorism. For the purposes of prevention, it is important to more clearly define the distinguishing features between terrorism and mass shootings that are otherwise motivated.

Both mass shootings and terrorism cause significant anxiety in America. Despite the growing frequency of mass shootings, they are still on the whole a poorly defined phenomenon, especially as distinguished from actual terrorism. One commonly used definition of a mass shooting come from an NYPD report, which requires the following elements be present: "(a) involved a firearm, (b) appeared to have struck random strangers or bystanders and not only specific targets, and (c) not occurred solely in domestic settings or have been primarily gang-related, drive-by shootings, hostage-taking incidents, or robberies."

Not all mass shootings are treated equally. The Pulse Nightclub Shooting was featured in Showtime dramatic mini-series The Comey Rule, which shows actor Jeff Daniels in a largely sympathetic portrayal of FBI Director James Comey touring the horrifically depicted scene while bodies lay *in situ* on the nightclub floor. Though understandable for the efficiencies required for dramaturgical acumen, it is worthy to note that this did not actually happen. James Comey did visit the Orlando area five days after the shooting, according to the FBI's own press releases to thank first responders and health care providers for often working above and beyond the expectations of their job descriptions in response to the event. However, this can also be viewed as part of the mythopoetic function of our culture to digest events that penetrate deeply into the collective consciousness. Not only has popular media engaged in such activity, but it was also directly Mateen's intent for society to do so. The phrase that "the personal is political" harkens back to the women's suffrage movement and is also applicable not only to considerations of the broad acceptance of the LGBTQ+ community, but intersectionalism in general. Having said all that, Mateen's credibility as a "cultural warrior", and therefore any claim to lethal action that could be even vaguely credited with political motives, is severely delegitimized by his deeply personal problems. A significant portion of mass shooters have a violent history. Indeed, this was the case with Mateen, whose marriage seemed to be ending in part at least due to his tendency for domestic violence. Journalists, the American people, but also the shooters have come to view coverage of rampage killings as tragically routine; this predictability results in contagion and encourages fame-seeking by the shooters themselves. One reason Mateen claimed to be a terrorist, may have been a desire that the public think of him as such, rather than the maladapted and sexually confused individual he really was. This would have been far more acceptable to the community he was part of. Although while researching the case, I found no evidence of pro-terrorist sentiment, there was significant anti-homosexual sentiment espoused even by his own father.

By placing the crime within a mythopoetic framework we can divorce it from geopolitical considerations. Still, it is not unworthy of note that a spectrum exists and that events such as these are best placed along it with some sense of nuance. The comfort we might find in isolating Omar Mateen as a crazed individual is not bolstered by any knowledge of global events such as they might occur. Rather, the intent should be an understanding of the factors that precipitated the Pulse Nightclub Shooting in order that future events such as these might be prevented, regardless of where they appear on the motivational spectrum. The failure to understand mass shooters, even with a certain empathy, creates allows us to create a scapegoat which while comforting is anti-productive. In dismissing mass shootings as incomprehensible tragedies or relegating them to war oriented thinking by labeling them terrorism, we miss potential opportunities to thwart them with greater efficacy. The derivation of the word gun comes from the Scandinavian Gunhildr, which means "battle-maiden." Gunhildr a possibly fictional figure from history's twilight, she was known for acts of extreme cruelty. Some mass shootings could be fueled by a warped perception of masculinity and power. Manifesting as a violent attempt to reclaim a perceived sense of dominance or prove sexual potency. In Mateen's case, this may have been connected to a history of homosexual activity, possibly at Pulse Nightclub itself.

The FBI interviewed Mateen on multiple occasions about potential terrorist ties, which Mateen would claim to have in various settings. While it could be considered to always be inappropriate to claim to have terrorist ties, Mateen made such claims at particularly inappropriate times. Such as when he was being vetted to be a policeman and later in a similar process for being an armed security guard. The company that ran a background check on Mateen apparently did so fraudulently as a matter of course, making it easy for him to go unnoticed. Mateen did travel to Saudi Arabia twice to perform the *umrah*, otherwise known as the 'small pilgrimage. Each trip lasted over a week, which is standard, although the *umrah* itself only takes a few hours to perform. It is possible but unknown if Mateen might also have traveled to the United Arab Emirates during one or both of these trips. Given what we know of Mateen, that he may attempted to get some terrorist training or make terrorist contacts is not unthinkable. We also know that Mateen tended to make a very poor impression. He may have amateurishly flailed about like a drug seeking pubescent in a bad part of town and accomplished little more than convincing anyone who might be such a contact that he was too volatile to deal with.

Still, it is interesting to note that his computer search history and phone records contained little to no evidence of any homosexual proclivity, although some people described Mateen as a regular and belligerent presence at the Pulse Nightclub among other gay establishments. This could be viewed as predatory stalking, but most predators do not wander into the middle of a herd and make themselves known. An explanation equally as likely, perhaps even more likely, was that Mateen was 'cruising'. Cruising is a term of art referring to gay men looking for sexual encounters that could be described as quick and discreet to the point of being anonymous. There is little doubt that some aspect of violence could have been blended with his sense of sexuality, nor is it unknown nor always unwelcome for some both within and without the gay community to 'like it rough'. Mateen was known to be using steroids, which is associated with risky sexual behavior and gay experimentation. Such subcultures often thrive in the shadows. Transactions are initiated with a glance or a gesture. Encounters may be utterly wordless. Nonetheless, Mateen made an impression. As usual it was not a good one.

Even if Mateen had learned techniques of online anonymity from terrorist sources, which are hardly required to learn them, that such hypothetical training was only applied to personal sexual gratification belies his stated political motivations. Such pursuits would appear to be central to his activities, rather than incident to his "terrorist" planning. Mateen never planned for any action other than the Pulse Nightclub. What threatened him most was not an international conspiracy against Muslims, but his own sexuality which put *him* in conflict with the Muslim faith as it is conceived in some more conservative circles of that community. Minority populations are disproportionately targeted by mass shootings, which show a correlation to violent political rhetoric in the public sphere. The apparent intent of such speech is to encourage those susceptible to its messages to commit violent acts, and is perhaps an even more effective mechanism than intended by it purveyors given how commonly it can be heard in our political discourse. Though Mateen's crime begs for the validation of terrorist elements, that appeal is *post hoc*. The motivation is not to fight a threat to the Muslim community, but to destroy those elements of his own identity threatened by the existence of his minority sexual desires. Because he could not cause the extinction of such feelings within himself, he sought to destroy them in familiar territory: a nightclub where he likely found the means to experience some of his fantasies. Destroying that was as close as he could get to destroying that part of himself. Mateen's claim was not a delusion, far less common in mass shootings than one might think, but a self-conscious lie he hoped others would believe.

Although ideology is the second most common motivation for mass shootings after fame-seeking, Mateen could be interpreted as a victim-specific shooter. This is the least common type. In such events the shooter intends to kill someone specific but kills any other people present in the pursuit, though this is admittedly an idiosyncratic interpretation of what happened at Pulse Nightclub. We will never have dispositive proof that he went to the Pulse Nightclub seeking a specific victim with whom he had a sexual liaison, but if we accept the theory of the crime as being less about his stated ideology and more about his sexual confusion it certainly becomes a possible scenario. LGBTQ+ nightclubs and bars are not unknown to have so-called "back rooms", where consenting adults may participate in relatively anonymous sex acts, or with known partners but with the added thrill of being in public. Whether Pulse Nightclub had such a backroom in indeterminate. What is known is that the club was cited for unpermitted work and renovations. Some of it, including an area outside a fire escape door that had been fenced off with eight-foot-high chain link, may have impeded patrons ability to escape. Police described a soft drink vending machine that had to be moved out of the entrance, at grave risk, before SWAT Teams could enter. Pulse Nightclub could have seen a body count after an electrical fire, much less a mass shooting. While according to the law such establishments as the Pulse Nightclub should be empty and shuttered by 2 am, it was not only at least at capacity but had a known history of going far over capacity. The point being that it is more plausible to imagine sex acts happening at a club which is already pushing the edges of legality. Mateen may well have engaged in such sex acts whether or not Pulse Nightclub did have a back room, as even restrooms can be used for encounters. Mateen's victim specific intent could have been painted with a broad brush, particularly if he were unclear on such a sex partner's actual identity, hidden as it could have been by institutional intent, darkness and intoxication.

Mateen's unwelcome sexuality, potentially, could be countered by use of a gun not just for self-destruction. Just as we project our own shadow and aggression onto Mateen, he projected it onto the community of sexual minorities. By exteriorizing them as an other, and viewing them as part and parcel of an American culture he views as a threat to the purity of Islam, he could effectively extinguish it not only in the world but in himself. We must wonder how often mass shooters act subconsciously to a felt sense of inadequacy. Many mass shooters have a history of being rejected by their peers. They may feel that inadequacy is only proven by a suicide, and so attempt to disprove it by mass murder prior to self-destruction. Most mass shooters kill themselves in less than five minutes after their rampage begin, and few willingly surrender to police.

In cases like these, it may be simplistic to view the gun as a simple tool intended to do a simple task.

Mateen's guns were perhaps more like submissive lovers. Objects of ultimate physicality, purpose and intent, yes, but also the only allies he finds in a lonely and frightening world. Beyond being a simple substitute for phallic virility, the guns were stalwart companions and fierce advocates. Form follows function in a gun no less than it does in our corporeal forms. The broad hips one might grasp in a succumbing a lover are paralleled by bump stocks, banana magazines and additional accoutrements known only to the most fanatic adherents to so-called "gun culture".

That Mateen claimed an explosive capability he did not have explicitly separates this from terrorism. Explosive vests and car bombs are not off the shelf capabilities the way guns are. Making them requires not only an expertise but a logistical support Mateen that were clearly absent.

Omar Mateen was not a terrorist, but rather a deeply disturbed individual with a lifelong history of violence, who had suffered a devastating personal loss in the failure of his marriage. His identification with international terrorism was in some ways a reaction to his own confused sexuality. He sought exterior destruction to legitimize his own self-destruction and throw others off of the scent of his hidden identity. His bluster about explosives indicates a certain self-awareness of his own incompetence and confusion.

In the pursuit of understanding, and

in understanding attempting to reduce, mass shootings, we can get so lost in the hope of an informative granularity that meaningful parallels are lost. At heart, murderousness and aggression are an inextricable part of the human experience whether it is acted upon or not. When we say this shooting is due to psychosis, this one is terrorism, this one is simple revenge, we can lose the thread that could lead us from the labyrinth. In the case of Omar Mateen, almost every element seems at least partially in play. An anti-social nature, cultural conditioning, personal loss, psychological confusion and simple hatred all seem to be in the mix. Synthesizing these elements holds promise, if not the promise of absolute revelation, then at least greater understanding. However, it may be as important to consider what is unknown or unclear as to consider what dispositive proof can be gleaned from each case. Real life is filled with unknown variables, and often questions that can never be satisfactorily answered.

Mass shootings are growing in number and lethality. Their prevention is complicated by the fact that shooters often have not had previous encounters with law enforcement, and in some cases where they have, they were cleared of wrongdoing. Solutions remain elusive without a more interventionist approach to possibly disturbed individuals, and greater vigilance by the community to identify those who may be verging into such deviantly murderous activity.

FROM SHERLOCK TO MURDERBOT

"You know my method. It is based on the obsevance of trifles.... I found the ash of a cigar, which my special knowledge of tobacco ash enabled me to pronounce as an Indian cigar. I have, as you know, devoted some attention to this, and written a little monograph on the ashes of 140 different varieties of pipe, cigar, and cigarette tobacco."

From this tiny bit of ash at a crime scene, which Sherlock Holmes can recognize on sight, he destroys a suspect's alibi in *The Boscombe Valley Mystery*, and, as always, pinpoints the murderer's identity. Though we all know these are fictitious stories, their popularity raised awareness of using crime scene analysis and the scientific method to help solve crimes. Some of Sir Arthur Conan Doyle's stories were even quite prescient. Holmes uses fingerprint analysis in *The Sign of the Four*, published in 1890, which Scotland Yard would not adopt until more than a decade later. The genre has only gained popularity since the world was first introduced to Sherlock Holmes, and he was even updated to a 21st century portrayal by actor Benedict Cumberbatch. In it Holmes still lives on Baker Street, seems to rely on illicit substance use and at least occasionally wears a deer stalker hat. Dr. Watson is still his only friend, and that sometimes begrudgingly .

J. Edgar Hoover in an undeniably remarkable figure if for no other reason than his nearly half century and the director of the Federal Bureau of Investigation. He also oversaw the agency during what is possibly the most intensive period of domestic surveillance by the government before the explosion of social media. While much of our current surveillance, known and unknown, was radically enhanced by both technological capabilities and fear in the aftermath of 9/11, for Hoover it was often quite personal. Much of it was also blatantly illegal. There is no good reason within the guardrails of the jurisprudence on issues of personal liberty to keep track of the sex life of Martin Luther King Jr. His aversion to the use of psychology can be deconstructed in light of its association at the time with the very same counter-cultural movements he was rabidly opposed to. Before then, the psychological movement started by figures like Freud and Jung, 'psychoanalysis' as it was called was originally either reserved for the very seriously impaired or even a bit of parlor trickery whereby the privileged would analyze each other over cigars and brandy. Early psychologists had very little interest in crime, many of whom looked down on Freud and Jung, although this popularity presaged the intuition that psychology was broadly applicable beyond questions of sanity. Hoover's contribution should not be readily dismissed, he professionalized what in some ways was a rogue agency, emphasized fingerprinting and established the first federal forensic science laboratory in 1932. Still, his legacy is a troubling one overall, and his failure to embrace the potential value of psychology is among the criticisms that can be legitimately levied against him. After his death, people at the agency and academia became freed to explore the subject of psychology within criminology and eventually the Behavioral Science Unit at the newly created FBI Academy in Quantico.

Humans have a negativity bias for very good reasons. Our ancestors who spent more time marveling over wildflowers than worrying about what might be hiding among them got eaten. That bias is so strong we have turned it into entertainment. Even the gentlest movies and books contain some level of conflict or there would be little drama to care about. Popularity of the genre should not be dismissed as prurient. Indeed, more than one amateur sleuth has cracked a case! True crime podcasts, books and documentaries proliferate well beyond their fictional counterparts, themselves innumerable. Nothing is more negative than malevolence. Far from its depiction in popular entertainment, forensic psychology is only rarely used for profiling *unknown* suspects and often enough is utterly useless to their identification and can even be counterproductive. In your average television show a crack psychologist, all but worshipped for their quirky genius by their colleagues, notices some detail in a crime scene in the first five minutes of the show. Before ten minutes are up they have a spot on description of the killer even though they have no idea who he really is, but by the half hour mark they're on his tail and have caught him, within five minutes he proudly confesses, sealing the deal. At the forty two minute mark we see the whole team cheerfully enjoying a beer together before returning home to their stable marriages where they apologize to their wife for how busy they've been for the past week catching this terrible killer. Such spouses are universally supportive. The next week they do the same thing all over again. While the description above is a parody of 'police procedurals' it is recognizable enough to have an intrinsic credibility. This not at all how real investigations work and it is even less how forensic psychology works.

When investigating peer reviewed literature on behavioral profiling the aspect that stands out is how extraordinarily dated much of it is. Many papers are from before the turn of the century.

Generally, forensic psychology prefers to use studies from within the last five years as it is more likely to stand up in court and less subject to challenges by other social scientists. This seems almost impossible to accomplish currently. Research subjects wax and wane in the attention they receive often in conjunction with available funding. According to the FBI's own website, their Behavioral Science Unit has not published anything since early in 2010. One rather obvious way to improve crime scene profiling would be to fund more studies of it! Unless we do, profiling in general may be relegated to the dust bin of history, and a potentially valuable tool could be lost. Profiling itself may have earned a bad name due to its association with racial profiling by which police may be more likely, as a for instance, to pull over minorities for minor traffic violations and may even make police more likely to escalate situations to where injuries and deaths can occur. New York's Stop and Frisk policy definitively showed a minority bias and was deemed unconstitutional (Thompson, 2013). Despite this it seems to be on the rise again. We could very much be throwing out the baby with the bathwater, leaving unsolved cases that might otherwise have been cleared.

Of greatest untapped potential in forensic psychology generally and crime scene analysis in particular is machine learning. The world is all aflutter over Artificial Intelligence, although according to chemist Dr. Leroy Cronin that may be overblown, who refers to it instead as "Automated Informatics" just to annoy his colleagues. His recent work on assembly theory seems quite applicable to criminology. The data sets around forensic psychology are enormous and growing every day. To my knowledge machine learning has not been applied to the vast majority of these data sets and *could* reveal unexpected correlations which *could* prove useful to criminologists. Depending on the methodology however, particularly the application of neural networks, we often get answers which though accurate, remain untraceable. The process by which the computer reaches its outputs from its inputs occurs within a black box. We do not know exactly the system reaches the conclusions it does despite their accuracy. There may be a significant amount of cultural resistance to such an application, nor would they be unlikely to stand up in court and perhaps that is as it should be. The risk of sacrificing our liberties to automated systems is too great and the fear of such is not unjustified. To give an example, perhaps a system fed thousands of crime scene photos as well as the characteristics of whoever was ultimately convicted of the crime could lead towards suspects either generally or specifically. However, AI is known to "hallucinate", giving occasionally wildly inappropriate answers such as a recent example of recommending the addition of glue to pizza sauce to keep the cheese from sliding off. Without corroborating evidence, machine learning alone could not, and absolutely should not, be used to convict someone of a crime. The potential here is at once both very hopeful and quite terrifying. To an extent, it is only a matter of time before that story gets fictionalized, and more generally it already has in abundance. Skynet, in the *Terminator* franchise centers around an AI that decides humans are irredeemably dangerous and must be eradicated. *The Matrix* has an essentially identical plot save that rather than eradication the Machines use people as batteries. In a more recent, and frankly more nuanced iteration Muderbot in *The Murderbot Diaries* combines noir detective stories with cyberpunk horror whereby a SecUnit android's failing 'governor module' leads it to try and a live a quiet life passing as a human while watching streaming dramas, but it keeps getting pulled into administering justice for stupid humans who always seem to be trying to get killed. Murderbot loathes humans. The astro-archaeologists he was randomly contracted to protect when his governor module failed, seem particularly dumb after discovering shocking aliens ruins that put them in conflict with vast corporate powers. Nonetheless, it rises to the occasion as best it can, complaining the whole time. "I can't even do the half-assed version of this stupid job if I have to talk to humans," it writes in its diaries. While it may seem tangential, we must wonder to if these stories might not be as prescient as Doyle was with fingerprinting. The idea that technology *will* radically alter our relationship to and understanding of justice is embedded in the current zeitgeist. Both the promise and the problems need to be worked out ahead of time as much as possible, and it is not at all clear that we intend to do so. Simply the anxiety, not at all unjustified, is a psycholegal question demanding address.

AMERICAN SNIPER

Chris Kyle was a highly decorated sniper with US Navy Seals. During four tours overseas he logged the most confirmed kills of any sniper in history. Afterwards, he not only wrote a training manual for future snipers, becoming chief instructor for snipers at the Naval Academy but also published a best selling autobiography about his experiences which was later adapted into an Academy Award winning movie starring the actor Bradley Cooper. Kyle struggled with the understandable burdens associated with his war fighting career, but translated that into a strong urge to help other veterans with similar struggles. Tragically, that all came to an end while he was at a shooting range with Eddie Ray Routh, a twenty five year old former marine whose family claims was struggling badly with his mental health. Routh had accompanied Kyle and Chad Littlefield to a Texas gun range for recreational shooting when Routh turned one of the guns on his companions killing them both.

While the burden of defending any client

accused of murder is very high, such issues are compounded when the victim was not only attempting to help the perpetrator, but are themselves exceptionally charismatic and well known. It is no exaggeration to say that Chris Kyle could be called a national hero. It is exceptionally difficult to reconcile Kyle's patriotism and charity with Routh's senseless betrayal. Juries are often loath to acquit on charges of homicide through an insanity plea based solely on the psychological distress of a perpetrator. The test for insanity in legal jurisprudence is extraordinarily high, as the perpetrator must have been in a state of mind where they were unable to appreciate the nature of the crime they have committed at the time of the incident. For Routh, the defense team must put into evidence as much as possible regarding Routh's deteriorating mental state as witnessed by his family and friends to persuade as many jurors as possible that he was not guilty due to insanity.

The legal definition of insanity for criminal defense has remained largely unchanged since the mid-1800s. Consider the vast evolution of psycholegal understanding. While our standards for legal insanity haven't significantly changed since the mid-1800s, a recent example in Arizona highlights the disconnect. Their Supreme Court revived an 1864 law setting the age of consent for women at ten. This was also around the time the US Supreme Court told Dredd Scott he had no right to sue for his freedom from slavery because he was not a person, he was property, rather directly resulting in the Civil War. These are concepts completely incompatible with modern psychology and legal principles, not to mention inimical to our basic sense of humanity. Proposals for the first defense based on temporary insanity faced significant public resistance a few years later, and attitudes have not changed much since. The concept of proportional mens rea has languished in obscurity since the 1950s. Our legal system operates with outdated notions of mental health. While the legal insanity criteria haven't budged since the mid-1800s, breakthroughs in psychology, neurology, and social sciences are painting a much more nuanced picture of the human mind. These discoveries are all very recent. Due to their foundation in empirical evidence and substantial probative value, their admission as evidence is practically inevitable.

Punishment's primary purpose is deterrence, and it is widely thought its effectiveness increases with severity. While the public desire for retribution exists, it's often outweighed by the need to effectively discourage crime. However, for individuals demonstrably incapable of understanding consequences or controlling criminal impulses, punishment becomes simply punitive suffering, raising potential constitutional concerns.

In the early 1920s, a group of distinguished

judges, lawyers, and law professors established the American Law Institute. They aimed to clarify core legal principles and reduce inconsistencies across jurisdictions. In the area of insanity, dissatisfied with the rigid 'all-or-nothing' insanity test, they proposed a framework for how mental illness could impact criminal responsibility and granted juries significant discretion in determining the level of mental impairment that could reduce or negate criminal liability. The central idea is that true moral culpability hinges on rationality at the time of the offense. While concerns exist that juries might misinterpret this flexibility, leading to malingering on the part of defendants and wrongful acquittals, perhaps a more significant worry lies in the damage to public trust caused by wrongful convictions and even future historians' opinions of the fairness of our current system.

The profound stigma surrounding mental illness discourages young adults from seeking help when symptoms first appear in early adulthood. People with mental illness can be especially critical of themselves, even more so than those around them. Training in mental healthcare doesn't eliminate ingrained biases – even specialists can hold them towards their patients. Our current legal system, where juries weigh mental illness in criminal cases, operates within a society deeply ingrained with stigma. While these decisions are instructed to consider only the most extreme cases, achieving truly fair deliberations amidst such widespread bias is a significant challenge if not perhaps impossible. Unfortunately, some attempts to address this issue, like public awareness campaigns, haven't shown consistent effectiveness and might even have the unintended consequences of making stigma worse. The pursuit of justice, undeniably, is a demanding and often uncomfortable endeavor. However, to call it just requires fairness as its core principle. An unfair system breeds not only non-compliance, but the very notion of following the law could become illogical.

Juries wield immense power over a case's outcome. A single juror dissenting against conviction leads to a mistrial. In some instances, this may trigger double jeopardy, permanently barring a retrial. Jury nullification empowers the jury to act as society's conscience, even when the prosecution presents a strong case. Historically, this principle played a role in the abolitionist movement, where juries sometimes refused to convict those who aided enslaved people seeking freedom. While jury nullification grants juries the power to acquit a defendant despite the letter of the law, it's a concept often met with resistance from prosecutors and judges. Although judges instructing against nullification constitute a constitutional error, successfully appealing such errors is uncommon. Exercising jury nullification can be difficult in practice, despite its legal existence. Reviving this longstanding tradition in jurisprudence presents a challenge. Coercing courts to accept a specific standard for nullification is unlikely. Legislative action might be necessary, even though jury nullification itself seems to be experiencing a resurgence.

Despite its extensive use, serious questions remain about so-called Scientific Jury Selection to the extent that the term itself has fallen out of favor. In some mock trials outcomes correlated to specific demographic or attitudinal factors were little better than random number generators. Indeed, demographic correlations to specific crimes has been shown to be not just divergent but oppositional to each other. There simply is no definitive manual that predicts human behavior. Having said that, given the defense approach is to assert not only that Routh was suffering from a significant decompensation of mental faculties, but that even in the absence of absolute insanity mental illness is given insufficient consideration, avoiding authoritarian personality types is likely imperative. Such information could be reasonably well gleaned from social media accounts. Authoritarianism is largely although not exclusively associated with conservative politics, and people with such a personality type are decidedly prone to convict. To try and fairly sum up the authoritarian attitude, rules exist for a reason and should not be readily ignored regardless of context.

Without meaning to impugn the enlightenment of the residents of the great state of Texas the defense team had an uphill battle with Routh's defense. Not only were they not allowed to speculate that even an insanity plea could see him serve what is effectively a life sentence in a secure psychiatric facility, but just days before *voir dire* the Governor of Texas declared it was "Chris Kyle Day" in his honor. Realistically, the best possible outcome for Routh may have been to avoid the death penalty. This occurred because the prosecution did not seek it, but it could be considered that the arguments for Routh's mental instability made by the defense did influence that outcome.

PADUCAH

School shootings seem to be an increasing problem even as the rate of violent crimes is generally declining. After such an event, a traumatized community is desperate for answers and to hold someone accountable. In the case of the shooting in Paducah, Kentucky in 1997 by Michael Carneal serious questions about the nation's culture arose, some of which were adjudicated. Since that time recognition and intervention into the lives of youth who may be at risk of perpetrating such an event have increased greatly. Further questions about partial responsibility by the parents have also been asked and answered. Few issues garner more national attention or cause as much heartbreak as a shooting at a school. In 2021 thirty-five of school shootings resulted in injuries or death and of the fifteen deaths that occurred in those incidents the majority were children. Communities are rocked by these incidents, with many questions arising, some of which are unanswerable. The injustice of a life cut short in such a violent manner leaves friends and family of the deceased traumatized for years, perhaps forever. Until recently, it seemed a near-evident assumption that our children were generally safe from real harm in a school setting.

Exactly what leads to these senseless tragedies is often quite difficult to discern. Some question whether popular media, which often depicts and sometimes glorifies violence, could be contributing to this terrible trend we might expect to hear about in the news at any time. The responsibility of the shooter's parents is increasingly asked by the public. Americans access to mental health care, considered to be in crisis particularly for the young , exacerbated by a shortage of qualified professionals is put into stark relief by such events. It is much easier to get access to the weapons themselves then perhaps it should be, in part due to an enthusiastic gun culture highly protective of what they see as their rights under the Second Amendment. However, citizens also have a right to a reasonable expectation of safety as provided by various parts of the government, including schools. Laws on both the state and federal level are trying to respond to this crisis, but there is little reassurance to be had that this trend will be stopped soon.

On January 21, 1860 In Todd County, Kentucky a son of the prominent Col. Elijah Sebree was shot and killed by another student. Other students had been teasing the perpetrator, saying the Colonel's son intended to do him harm, maybe even kill him. The perpetrator retrieved a gun from home and returned to the school, and killed him. Both the victim and the perpetrator are unnamed by the Daily Dispatch where it was front page news on January 26, 1860. Nor is there any mention of consequences that may have occurred. However, it is the first recorded instance in the United States of a school shooting committed by a minor student. Although a different incident, also in Kentucky, is often cited as the first school shooting, the perpetrator in that case was 28 years old.

Less than a hundred miles away, but more than a hundred years later, tragedy would strike again. It may be unfair to assign to Kentucky such a seminal place in this grim history, but it is not inaccurate. Comment on these origins risk prejudicial assumptions.

In 1997, the small Kentucky village of Paducah was marked by tragedy. Freshman Michael Carneal opened fire on his fellow students killing three people and injuring five others. The shocking act created a national debate about school security, mental health and particularly issues around violent media, books and video games. Decades later it remains unclear what his motivations were. An isolated boy with a troubled home life, he may have been bullied and psychiatric evaluations indicated he might suffer from schizophrenia. A sentence of life imprisonment with the possibility of parole after 25 years was given by the court on the assumption he could be rehabilitated through treatment while he was in jail. Survivors and victim's families soundly opposed granting him parole, highlighting the heinousness of his crime and his future risk to the community.

The Kentucky Parole Board disallowed Carneal's release thus condemning him to incarceration for life. The decision reflects how long-lasting the Heath High School shooting effects have been and how severely society views such acts. This is hardly a settled matter however, and it compels us to confront mental disease complexities alongside challenges of balancing rehabilitation and public safety, among many other issues.

In 1999, lawyer Jack Thomson represented families of victims who sued video game publishers, pornographic websites and two movies' producers for a total of $33 million. The contention was that violent contents from these media sources made Michael Carneal kill. Thompson himself and future US Attorney General John Ashcroft believed that the video games Carneal played not only made him an expert marksman but contributed to his desire to commit a mass shooting at his school. However, the lawsuit was dismissed three years later in 2002 when the court decided that there was not enough evidence linking his love of violent video games and media with the crime he perpetrated. The family agreed to pay $42m dollars in 2000 but also claimed not to have any assets to compensate victim's families.

In Carneal's locker that day was a book called "Rage" which was written under the pseudonym Richard Bachman by the well-known author Stephen King. The main character is Charlie Decker, an angry teen who shoots his algebra teacher, Miss Underwood, and holds his entire class hostage at gunpoint. Written from Charlie's viewpoint, the book unveils his underlying rage as he remembers certain episodes from his past. He had felt abused and frustrated by what he saw as power-hungry teachers. Charlie also makes sure that his fellow students come face to face with their own insecurities while they are held hostage. The book can hardly be said to glorify violence any more than Stephen King's book about vampires glorifies vampires. Charlie is the object of horror but also seeks instead to understand why such anger exists and what such anger can lead to. Stephen King admitted to feeling haunted by Carneal's shooting. King called his publisher and demanded that Rage be withdrawn from publication. The publisher granted his request. King never openly held his book responsible for the shooting though he acknowledged the potential impact it could have on a disturbed mind. To be fair, before Carneal's crime, school shootings were less of a problem in America and had not yet created the moral panic that exists today. Though a gun owner himself, King has supported stricter gun control policies since then. King chose to take responsibility for his work, but not the shooting itself, while advocating a wider approach to dealing with youth violence.

Craving connection with others is a fundamental human desire, and a big part of that is finding people we identify with. Our admiration extends to those who excel in our fields, or otherwise make meaningful contributions to culture and politics. It can be a healthy source of inspiration, especially when we see someone overcome challenges and can relate them to our own troubles. Indeed, religions often encourage identification with central exemplary figures, speaking to the power of this sense of connection. Identification can take a dark turn though. DeWayne Craddock, a civil engineer, opened fire at his Virginia Beach workplace in 2019, killing 12 people after emailing his resignation letter. Analysis after the fact revealed Mr. Craddock had what in retrospect was an unhealthy fixation on the DC Comics character Deadshot. Both Craddock and Deadshot are Black men highly critical of what they perceive as societal injustices. In both comics and the movie "Suicide Squad," Deadshot is perhaps the most lethal assassin in the world. While some superheroes can fly or have uncanny strength, Deadshot's ability with a gun verges on the supernatural. Craddock honed his weapon expertise through extensive military training, and additionally shot guns recreationally, likely contributing to the high death toll. Enjoying comics is hardly indicative of criminality, but the intensity of Craddock's interest was unusual for a man in his 40s. Culture often portrays men as responding violently to threats against their identity or honor, and in some cases does glorify such violence. Popular media reinforces this narrative with countless examples. In the case of Michael Carneal, it is unfair to try and blame Stephen King for his actions. Ron and Dan Lafferty claim they were inspired to kill their brother's wife and young daughter by their interpretation of The Book of Mormon so the source of murderous inspiration can be anything. Though King's book is disturbing, it is horror fiction, and of course meant to be disturbing. Carneal's excessive identification with the character of Charlie Decker removes no blame from him nor does it place it on Stephen King. Perhaps easy answers remove some of the pain from such tragedies, but the empirical evidence does not support them in this case.

The connection between violent video games/media and school shootings is unclear, and cuts to the heart of First Amendment rights. Indeed, even though citizens play more violent videogames than ever before overall rates of violent crime in America have dropped substantially since the 1990's. Violent media may increase aggression according to some studies, but it is unlikely they are solely responsible for school shootings. Mental health issues, access to mental health care, social isolation, bullying and access to guns are likely more salient risk factors.

The question of whether a family should be responsible for their children when they commit a mass shooting is a pressing one. A parent is supposed to supervise their child and be vigilant about their access to guns, to teach them an understanding of gun safety and help a child develop a moral compass. There are arguments against holding parents criminally and financially liable for a child's mass shooting case. Proving that a parent knowingly or negligently supported his child's violence can be a high prosecutorial burden. However, focusing on parental liability could incentivize a more interventionist approach when warning signs emerge. To date, no specific federal law holds parents directly accountable for a child's mass shooting. Civil lawsuits have been filed against the parents of perpetrators by the parents of victims, as in the case of Carneal, but historically they have a low success rate because of the difficulty of proving through a preponderance of the evidence that negligence was involved. Still, some states do have laws that make a parent financially responsible for property destroyed by a minor child if the child's intent is malicious, as discussed below. These laws could soon be applied to mass shootings.

Ethan Crumbley attacked Oxford High School in Michigan during November 2021, using weapons he had acquired from his parent's collection of firearms, resulting in multiple deaths. His parents, Jennifer and James Crumbly, were found criminally liable for his actions after ignoring several warnings from school officials regarding his conduct and concerns about his mental health. Their evidence included violent sketches he drew specifically of shooting other people, which the parents dismissed. The jury found Crumbleys had failed to properly secure their firearms or supervise his use and access to them. Ignoring these warning signs, combined with providing him access to guns constituted criminal negligence according to the prosecution. The jury agreed. They were both charged with four counts of involuntary manslaughter. Jennifer and Jason Crumbley both received ten to fifteen years in prison, which is the highest sentence ever given for an involuntary manslaughter conviction. After that case, there is a possibility of similar legal charges in future cases against parents who don't act when their child shows tendencies to become violent and has access to guns.

Childhood is a challenging experience for everyone. The body is constantly changing, we are emerging into an awareness of ourselves and finding our niche in the social strata. For minors who become school shooters, there are often similarities which are difficult to ignore, and yet that is often exactly what happens. Although, a quarter of children show signs of mental illness, only a quarter of those who do get treatment. Of those rare few who become school shooters, they are sometimes not merely isolated or lonely, but are being actively rejected by their peers. Beyond their social milieu however, they commonly exhibit extreme behaviors such as a deep fascination with violent historical figures and weaponry to the extent that they will do class assignments and even class presentations on the subject. This can be exactly the reason that they become socially isolated. However, not all school shooters fit the stereotype of the mentally ill bullied loner with a poor home life. Still, in most cases, the student involved has shown some threatening behavior beforehand, making threat assessment an important tool for prevention. Studies to date have not found a definitive profile for school shooters, but some common personality traits are narcissism, poor anger management and a lack of empathy. In analyzing the events leading up to a school shooting, perpetrators usually encountered some sort of stressor, displayed antisocial behavior, selected a target and acquired firearms in that order. Possibly the most effective time for intervention is just as some stressor is identified rather than further into their process.

Assessing the future dangerousness of a minor who has perpetrated a school shooting is no easy task, and some might be forgiven for automatically assuming the irredeemable nature of such offenders. Nonetheless, in *Miller v. Alabama* the Supreme Court has established the right of all juvenile offenders to have an individualized sentencing hearing where they may present possible mitigating factors that could lead to a reduced sentence compared to an adult offender. Predictions of future dangerousness are often required by courts, but such methods as they currently exist may result not only in a disproportionate number of false positives thereby causing unnecessary incarceration, but also comparatively rarer false negatives which nonetheless result in significant public outrage when they occur. The debate over the efficacy of unstructured clinical assessments in such cases has been in existence since the mid-20th century, but actuarial methodologies remain far from foolproof and show no signs of any ability to predict future dangerousness with absolute certainty.

In contrast to traditional law enforcement's reactive approach to crimes, which comes after the fact, Threat Assessment and Management (TAM) tries to proactively prevent violent events. School shootings, which have become a sad reality, are of particular interest and seem to be on the rise. TAM is crucial in schools, where faculty and staff have a responsibility to safeguard students. Other tools like the Comprehensive School Threat Assessment Guidelines (CSTAG) have been developed to distinguish serious threats from less concerning ones. Only 1% of at-risk students analyzed by CSTAG committed any violence, with none causing serious injuries. While some flagged students might be expressing frustrations typical of adolescence, it's important to note their graduation rate is 83%, and though lower than average still shows a positive outcome for the vast majority. A lot of overlap exists between school shootings and suicidal ideation and actions. Possibly a program meant to identify children at high risk of suicide. Suicides are far more common than school shooters, and attention paid to that issue would also identify those in the latter category without giving them the inauspicious label of being a threat.

Would-be school shooters often exhibit "leakage", meaning they signal their intent to peers, sometimes through social media. Anonymous tip lines can be crucial in catching such threats. A school's climate heavily influences reporting. Students are less likely to report threats in environments where teachers are perceived as unsupportive or where rules are thought to be applied unfairly.

Even as our crime rate continues to decline, concerns about crime are only heightened in the country by the numerous stories we hear daily about particularly horrifying events. Of those, although statistically rare, are mass shootings within our schools. Especially when perpetrated by minors, questions arise about the violence easily found in our popular media and whether individuals with mental health problems are being properly dealt with. The efficacy of school safety programs, gun control laws and the availability of powerful weaponry are contrasted by the truncated lives of dead children.

After such an event has occurred, the questions of what to do next are hardly silenced. The raging against the tragedy does not diminish with time, and forgiveness is usually in short supply. The United States continues to sentence mentally ill children to life without parole in many jurisdictions despite increasing calls to recategorize youthful offenders as capable of rehabilitation. While public safety is undoubtedly important, human liberty and the interests of justice are only partially addressed by retribution. It is possible we are scapegoating mentally ill children, who do not have the information processing capacity to be deterred by harsh sentences, for the failures of their elders in not creating a safer and more equitable world for them to grow up in.

Unfortunately, there is no reason to expect that school shootings will cease at any point in the foreseeable future. Indeed, there is a very high likelihood that one has occurred on this very day, although they are now so common that only the worst of them will make the news. For now, our reaction is almost exclusively punitive, and efforts to expand the sphere of liability may or may not achieve the intended results. Possibly, interventions earlier on with at risk youth will not only save possible victims, but possible perpetrators as well. For now, as Americans send their children off to school every day, mostly they can hope for luck that if something does happen at their school, their own child will not be involved.

POOLS OF BLOOD

SUFFER THE LITTLE CHILDREN

Few issues are more heartrending than the emergence of psychiatric disorders in children, particularly when those conditions have a high likelihood of eventually running them afoul of the law. Among the most worrisome for its potentially very poor prognosis is conduct disorder. Though known to be the second most common of psychiatric disorders in children, it ranked seventh for those youth who actually receive treatment. Though its exact conversion rate to full psychopathology is unknown, it shares many traits in common such as Callous-Unemotional affect, and in recent decades has become the focus of significant research into earlier detection of psychopathic personalities. Although the majority of children diagnosed with conduct disorder will adjust to more prosocial behaviors by adulthood, an earlier onset or greater severity of antisocial behavior predicts a greater chance of emergent criminality and substance abuse disorders. A poor home environment lacking warmth and acceptance, sometimes coupled with excessively authoritarian parenting practices, correlates to a higher incidence and severity of conduct disorder. In many cases, perhaps all, the fault does not lie with the child alone.

According to the DSM-5 Conduct Disorder occurs in roughly 4% of children and is defined as a problem of serious impulse control, emotional dysregulation and a tendency to violate the rights of others. Though it is very rare for conduct disorder to first emerge in adulthood, it is also a precursor diagnosis to Anti-Social Personality Disorder should the symptoms persist past age 18.

Aggression is a common feature of conduct disorder, though its expression can vary widely and be directed at authority figures such as parents or teachers, peers, animals or even property. Depending on whether the aggression tends to be impulsive or premeditated, different but significant anomalies have been observed in the neuroanatomy of children with conduct disorders as compared to healthy controls. The likelihood and severity of both types of aggression are correlated with callous-unemotional traits. Callous-unemotional traits appear to have the greatest persistence over time. Additionally, children with conduct disorder have a high risk of developing a wide variety of other disorders in adulthood including psychosis and substance abuse disorders.

There exists a therapeutic pessimism

regarding the treatment of severe conduct disorder. However, such pessimism could be viewed as self-defeating and even inappropriate given the possibility of future advances in our understanding not only of psychology but also neurology and even the social sciences. It is a bit early to concede defeat and merely relegate difficult children to eventual management by the criminal justice system. Very few difficult problems have been solved by simply lamenting how difficult they are.

Every period in history brings its unique challenges. In relation to childhood conduct disorder those include access to alcohol as well as a variety of other illicit substances and of course the internet. Youths have a natural tendency to seek autonomy, to distrust what they are told and to lack insight into how they are contributing to their own problems; all these natural tendencies are heightened in those with conduct disorders and coupled with the lack of self-efficacy inherent to the condition. This can lead to very poor outcomes. The use of intoxicating substances exists as a human universal and has widely varying degrees of cultural acceptance often dependent on peer and cohort exposure. The majority of children with conduct disorders have tried alcohol and or other illicit substances before the age of 12. In one study of juvenile offenders with conduct disorders 17% had used alcohol before the age of 10, and for a third of those with such premature exposure they reported frequent alcohol use by the age of 13. Children subject to abuse have an even higher likelihood of substance use and the earlier such use begins the more frequently they will eventually use such substances. The more often such children interact with law enforcement the greater the variety of substances they are likely to try. It may well be that the attempt to manage these issues as a matter of criminal delinquency is counterproductive.

Though such concerns have begun only in the past few decades, social media is providing children and youths with conduct disorders a fresh venue not only to perpetrate their aggression on others but to suffer abuse themselves online, where they suffer a much higher chance of both than children without conduct disorders. Such acts may be encountered or committed with absolute anonymity, and the widespread use of advanced phone technology can make this a seemingly inescapable problem. For those who commit so-called "cyberbullying" the number of times they are confronted with their behavior is exceedingly small. These technologies are subject to very little regulation, and one might expect the parental supervision of such online activity in dysfunctional homes to be intermittent when it exists at all. Regardless of the benefits such innovations have provided us, it must be acknowledged that a dark side exists, and is especially damaging to our most vulnerable children.

While legitimate concerns and understandable frustrations exist, abandoning difficult children to be dealt with by a strictly punitive criminal justice system is nothing short of the most reprehensible betrayal. Children do not construct society, adults do. The difficulty of finding effective treatment does not excuse the paucity of its attempted application. If anything, especially given the high stakes of poor outcomes, resources and research should be invigorated. New social systems and novel interventions must be constructed and deployed with greater urgency than is currently extant. We were all children once, thrown into an incomprehensible world, with gifts and deficits not of our own choosing. For those whose circumstances and embodiment are less than ideal, more effort should be made, not less.

GUILTY MINDS

Among the ways in which crime can be reduced voluntary legal compliance by the community may have superior efficacy. However, a number of factors dissuade people from cooperation with the criminal justice system, not the least of which could be attitudes about being tough on crime. Claims are made as to the value of deterrence with little empirical evidence to support them. This essay proposes potential innovations toward the end of greater legal compliance by the public, some of which are traditions well ensconced in jurisprudence, but anemic in practice and deserving of reexamination.

The law recognizes proportionality in criminal liability in part through the concept of *mens rea*, or guilty mind. This is particularly true in cases of homicide, although murder can be seen as a proxy for all crime, as what is true for the most extreme crime is likely true for crime in general. Particularly in reference to issues of remorse and compliance. Among the issues that can effect mens rea are considerations of mental illness which were largely formulated well over a century ago. The law has hardly kept pace with the science surrounding it, to put it mildly.

Issues that deter legal compliance have myriad etiologies, and some attitudes are deeply entrenched in certain communities where criminal justice is seen as excessively harsh to the point of being oppressive. No quick fixes are proposed here, and they are probably impossible in any case. This is likely the work of generations and will involve significant cultural changes not only by the law-breaking but also by the law-abiding.

In order to best refract backwards from a theoretical supposition it is often convenient to start with the most extreme examples if for no other reason than the attention they garnish. In the case of homicides this height, or this depth depending on how you look at it, is expressed in the real world by homicides committed as those we would label psychopathic. Psychopaths simultaneously appear both sane and insane. The most terrifying of them all are extraordinarily organized, which stands in stark contrast to how gruesome the damage they inflict is. Although what we call a psychopath is a lingua franca of our everyday lives, and the colloquialism has a certain value, its specific and extreme expressions are the cases that haunt our discipline. From the current psycholegal perspective such killers are fully responsible for their actions, even if their underlying motives verge on the unimaginable due to their horrific nature. *If* there is an argument to be made here for empathy, leniency and forgiveness, then such things are applicable anywhere. Our fascination with these "psychokillers" is culturally broad. Lessons may exist within worth learning.

Although recency can have value, especially in forensic arenas where evidence-based assertions gain primacy, the works of Sigmund Freud are seminal. The legal recognition of of the concept of transference informs the ethical standards by which psychiatrists and psychologist may be judged and have been judged in cases of even criminal liability. Freud is sometimes called humanity's third insult after Copernicus and Darwin, a comparison he made himself. Not only was our world not the center of the universe and our resemblance to primates not coincidental, but our firm belief we ride astride the great mount of free will has very little basis in fact. Freud said that much of our behavior arises from a deep unknowable well of subconscious drives we are in thrall to. Largely, our behavior happens, and we justify it afterwards. This is quite insulting to humanity generally, particularly in those cases where justification after the fact verges on the unimaginable. It is also deeply terrifying and not entirely unjustified.

Innovation is often the result of the uncomfortable coming together of the old and the new. The highest technology device the average person encounters will use the Latin alphabet and

Arabic numerals. Jurisprudence is similar, with some precepts dating back to ancient times. The salient question then becomes does an evolving sense of decency have vulnerabilities in the face of a superior understanding. In other words, can evidence influence the outcome of a trial? The answer is, of course, it is the only thing that is supposed to. It is then that the efficacy of psychological evidence becomes of paramount importance, but psychology is no stranger to controversy.

By virtue of its irreversible consequences, homicide—the unlawful taking of another person's life—is generally deemed the most serious of all crimes. Cases involving excessive cruelty, which target innocent victims and are characterized by random violence tend to be the most difficult to defend and often receive the severest punishments, including death. Nevertheless, an adversarial justice system ensures an effective defense for everyone. This defense should utilize new scientific discoveries and any ethical issues concerning individual rights as they pertain to the accused. Moreover, it also makes imperative broader questions of reforming judicial, penal, and legislative systems in order to bring about true justice.

Some suggest a radical departure, whereby we view all forms of violence as a public health concern that requires treatment and prevention instead of punishment. Although not feasible for many cases this raises questions about whether punishment is really an effective way of preventing recidivism. Research shows that punishment may not affect those who have severe mental illness. They cannot be deterred in the same way as other people. If the death penalty is about vengeance instead of justice its use becomes questionable. While severe punishments may appease public outcry, a more productive approach might involve rehabilitation and risk assessment within secure facilities.

When a person has experienced Adverse Childhood experiences, and develops neuroanatomical and or biochemical anomalies violent behavior is often an unsurprising outcome. Therefore, while such problems do not deliver criminal actors from the aspirational value of free will inherent in the law, acknowledging such deficits as possible mitigating factors is all but demanded by considerations of fairness.

In the course of a citizen's kinds of exposure to government, ones involving the police are likely the most prevalent. They certainly occur more than with politicians or other government functionaries. The sound of police sirens near and far is so common as to be considered unnoteworthy. Of all those interactions police are also unique in their ability and license to use lethal force. Police could be considered the government's ground game. As such they are subject to the closest scrutiny and debate by the populace. In considering how to increase public legal compliance, particularly of those who have committed a criminal act, the deportment of police is paramount. Recent media attention about police behavior has brought such concerns forward and significant questions exist about whether efforts to improve relations between the police and the public have been effective. While no readily available studies seem to exist about the factors which could lead a criminal to surrender to the police or to act cooperatively with police in an investigation, numerous proxies do exist from which we could extrapolate why citizens *do not* do so.

Of significant moment is the debate about the increasing militarization of the police. While being Black correlated with increased cynicism about police in general and particularly as to whether the police have become too militarized, older age and political conservatism nearly negates the effect size of this sentiment. However, even among those who do hold the police as having higher legitimacy and do support militarization those asked to describe police in uniforms and carrying gear more congruent with a military style described them as unapproachable, potentially untrustworthy and even immoral. While the argument is made that such militarized police deter crime and increases officer safety, empirical evidence does not uphold this assertion. At least some of this increase in military style gear and accoutrement was inspired by the so-called "War on Drugs", an explicitly military attitude, but the attitudes of the officers themselves towards perpetuating that particular struggle in such a manner is waning rapidly and broadly seen as ineffective. While there can be no question that certain circumstances require special weapons and tactics, having this as the default presentation of the police to the public may be doing more harm than good.

There is no question but that policework is one of the most stressful jobs in our society. The vast majority of police will encounter situations they themselves describe as traumatic. Over the course of their career a significant number of police will have symptoms of Post-Traumatic Stress Disorder. Despite all of this, significant stigma exists within the culture of police against mental illness or seeking help for psychic distress. Maladaptive responses to stress and mental illness are also strongly correlated with police misconduct and other poor outcomes. Negative interactions with police increase the public's cynicism, derailing the likelihood of cooperation and compliance. Such interactions seem to occur disproportionately in minority communities despite the insistence of many police that they take a colorblind approach to all interactions with the public, and may even arise from a subconscious tone of voice on the part of both parties which is not easily controlled. Without addressing such serious concerns truly effective police reform may be unachievable.

A different model of policing does exist. Community policing involves greater transparency, community involvement and the aggressive delivery of support services to socioeconomically disadvantaged areas. Such a system was used successfully for almost 20 years in Chicago, but sadly changes in leadership to those who actively disparaged it led to budget cuts and the collapse of the effort. A different effort in Los Angeles was also undertaken with mixed results, however returning to more frequent arrests did not address apparent shortcomings in the program. The model has hardly been abandoned though. In Troy, New York where this author currently resides, Project Sentinel has just been initiated in the hope of reducing a recent spike in violent crime committed by juvenile offenders. In contrast to the intimidating name, public statements by government officials promise to send the same police officers into the same neighborhoods which they will travel by foot and bicycle as opposed to patrol cars. Rather than warning of swift and severe punishment, new programs for at risk youth are being emphasized, and promises to listen to the concerns of members of the community are being made. One can hope this will lower the incidence of violent crimes in the area, but attitudes can be slow to change, and it is unlikely changes in policing will see immediate effects. In all likelihood, generations of effort will be required.

In a fascinating study of graffiti in Germany, draconian attempts at deterrence may have been demonstrated to have had the opposite of their intended effect. Public officials felt the problem of graffiti was out of control and changed the offense in some cases from a misdemeanor to a felony, greatly increasing potential penalties. Patrols specifically seeking to thwart and arrest graffiti artists were launched. Contrary to expectations graffiti seemed *to increase*. The issue of defiance is perhaps understudied, and causation requires us to speculate. Psychologically though, a community that feels itself specifically targeted and repressed by a certain law, in this case "sprayers", may be *more* inclined to break that law rather than less. Indeed, several sprayers reported that not only the excitement gained from creating graffiti but their personal reputation rose from doing it, the latter even more so if they were caught and punished. How tragic it would be if young people in particular were using hard drugs, killing each other and going to prison simply for the "juice" associated with defying the law. The concern should be the effect of a law, not its intent, nor public approval for "getting tough".

Daryl Reynard Atkins was a man with a long violent history who had been sentenced to death for the murder of Eric Nesbitt. However, he had an IQ of 59 points which occurs in less than 1% of the population, classifying him as mentally retarded. The American Association of Mental Retardation defines the condition as one of "significantly subaverage general intellectual functioning that is accompanied by significant limitations in adaptive functioning in at least two of the following skill areas: communication, self-care, home living, social/interpersonal skills, use of community resources, self-direction, functional academic skills, work, leisure, health and safety." Due to a wave of states independently enacting legislation that expressly prohibited the use of capital punishment on the mentally retarded, Atkins was brought before the Supreme Court who stated that due to society's evolving standards of decency, as indicated by the legislative actions, such executions should be prohibited under the Eighth Amendment. Punishment primarily exists as a deterrent to would-be criminals, which is considered more true when the punishment is more severe. The public need for retribution is at least partially obviated by the greater need for effective dissuasion. In those cases where a defendant is categorically incapable of processing such information or controlling the urges that result in criminality, punishment is merely unnecessary suffering and therefore unconstitutional. This could by hypothetical extension apply, not merely to those with an intellectual disability facing the death penalty, but to all those who may be deemed less than fully competent but who do not meet the legal criteria of insanity and face high-stakes penalties short of execution. In the absence of legislative action, it may be up to juries to indicate the evolving standards of decency. Somewhat dishearteningly, serious questions have arisen about whether *Atkins* is being properly applied, as what is known as the Flynn effect has seen a general rise in IQ scores which have not been taken into account , and that in some cases simple competence to stand trial has been improperly substituted for a true *Atkins* determination.

The American Law Institute was founded in the early 1920's by prominent figures within the field (American Law Institute, 2024). Their mission was to clarify fundamental principles of law to diminish jurisdictional variations in outcomes and understandings of jurisprudence. In the case of insanity, they proposed their own rubric of how mental illness could effect criminal liability, in large part due to dissatisfaction with the all-or-nothing tendency of the insanity test extant both then and now. Although specifically and questionably so-called psychopathic behavior was excluded from consideration it does allow juries absolute discretion to decide what would constitute a sufficient impairment that could serve to reduce or eliminate an individual's criminal liability. The central idea is that one can only be moral if at the time of the offense they are rational.

While legitimate concerns exist that such infinite discrimination by a jury could lead to an increase in malingering and wrongful acquittals perhaps of greater concern is the damage done to society's trust in government and the criminal justice system by wrongful convictions.

The stigma against mental illness is profound and can deter people from seeking help for it as it emerges in early adulthood. In many cases, no one is harder on the mentally ill than those who recognize they have one. Even healthcare workers specifically trained to work with the mentally ill are not immune from such prejudices. It is impossible to imagine in such a milieu that our courts, or the juries who decide criminal liability, currently give sufficient deliberation to questions of mental illness especially when they instructed not to save in the most extreme cases. A cultural problem so broad and deep is not easily fixed. In point of fact, some evidence has shown that efforts to reduce the stigma around mental illness, such as public awareness efforts, are largely ineffective and may even exacerbate the problem. Regardless, no one said the pursuit of justice would be easy, or comfortable, but it can hardly be said to be deserving of the name if it is not fair. If it is not fair, then compliance with the law is not only to be unexpected, but it could also be considered unwise.

Juries already have tremendous power in the outcome of a case. If even a single juror refuses to convict, a mistrial is declared and, in some cases, will trigger double jeopardy making a new trial impossible. Even if the prosecution has proven its case, jury nullification allows the public to serve as society's conscience as happened many times when juries refused to convict abolitionists who helped slaves escape capture. Nullification, however, is not popular with prosecutors and judges for obvious reasons, and though clearly a constitutional error when a judge gives instructions against nullification, such errors rarely result in a successful appeal. Arguably, jury nullification can barely be said to exist in practice at all. Reinvigorating this long tradition in jurisprudence is hard to imagine without coercing courts to adhere to the standard, but without legislative action it may be necessary although nullification itself may be on the rise.

Israel Keyes may be the most organized serial killer that has ever been discovered, which makes one of the most shocking aspects of his case how many things he did that are difficult understand outside of the idea that he was trying to get caught. The idea that all serial killers are incapable of remorse is brought into question by an informal study that showed approximately 2.3% of serial killers turned themselves and expressed remorse. Nor does that account for those serial killers, perhaps in a fog of anosognosia (defined as a clinical lack of self-awareness), who subconsciously did things to end their horrid careers. Keyes may well fit this bill. Still young and very strong, his killing career could have lasted indefinitely were it not for acts that maximized the possibility of his interception. For someone as apparently intelligent and organized as Keyes was, it is difficult to ascribe error or oversight to these acts. While it is very true that psychopathy is often associated with brazenness and insouciance, many serial killers go to greater lengths to hide their identities, if not always their crimes, than any other type of murderer might be expected to do. The case of headless woman found in California in 2011 who could only recently be identified by advances in genetic science and had never even been reported missing is one example. In some cases, serial killers are known to seem to flaunt the failures of police to trace them, such as in the case of the Zodiac Killer. Israel Keyes made "mistakes" your average internet scam artist would be embarrassed by. However, a different interpretation is possible which paints Keyes as inescapably enthralled to his own subconscious: both when he killed and possibly when he may have been trying to be stopped.

Around the United States remain undiscovered "murder kits" buried, hidden and preplaced in safety orange five-gallon buckets that Israel Keyes assembled for his crimes. These would be set about, and then Keyes would leave the area without committing a crime, perhaps to avoid detection. He drove extensively reconnoitering areas. Some of these kits have been found though it is suspected many more have not. Some may even contain evidence in unsolved cases. The active file against Israel Keyes ended with his suicide. During interrogation he claimed he had around 50 victims, but it is what he did with his last three that led to a capture that was nearly inevitable. Keyes extensively scouted for places where victims might be kidnapped from, different places where murdering them would be unlikely to be detected and other places where the remains could be hidden. These different spots were spaced geographically distant from each other. He liked water.

Samantha Koenig was kidnapped from her job as a barista on security camera by Israel Keyes and taken to his nearby home where he lived with his 10-year-old daughter and longtime girlfriend. In his unheated garage he raped and strangled her, later dismembering her body and putting it through an ice fishing hole in a nearby lake. However, between these two acts which show the intent of concealing the crime, he went on a Caribbean cruise with his daughter and left Ms. Koenig's frozen body in his garage. After returning suntanned and rested, he partially thawed her enough to sew her eyes open and pose her holding a newspaper as proof of life. He used this picture to demand a ransom of $30,000 to be deposited to her account *so that he could access it with her debit card*. Despite Keyes having a somewhat rural childhood and youth as part of a White

Christian Nationalist community, he was in many ways quite sophisticated in the use of the internet. Imagining him as a hapless hayseed killer is deeply contradicted by other evidence. Nonetheless, Keyes continued to use this card. First detected in Arizona, he basically used the card every time he stopped for gas. In many cases using drive up automated teller machines which captured his car and license plate behind him. He was intercepted in Lufkin, Texas and arrested without incident. His car was full of cash, weapons and murder kits in orange buckets. Faced with the video of Samantha Koenig's abduction Keyes instantly demurred. "Well," he is reported to have said, "I guess I might as well tell you everything."

Keyes lied. He did not tell them everything. What he did tell them about was another murder of a middle-aged couple in a small town this author is very familiar with called Essex, Vermont: Bill and Lorraine Courier. Within this current context elucidating the details of that case and extrapolating nuanced psychological insights becomes redundant if you take as a given that Keyes abducted and murdered two people on a day where their absence would be noticed immediately in such an intimate company town where IBM is the largest employer, and neither of the Courier's had hardly missed a day in decades. The day after they were reported missing, Keyes was seen by a neighbor of the Courier's driving their car in the area. A fearless indifference to consequences does not obviate their expectation, nor their perceived desirability by some aspect of the psyche which may not be self-consciously apparent. Sometimes humans act without awareness, but rarely without purpose.

Teleogically Keyes may have been trying to protect his daughter. He told the police what little he did in the hope of receiving a swift date for execution and as little media attention as possible, specifically so his daughter would not suffer the consequences of his actions. That is a very empathetic desire to the extent that almost anyone might wish it into being for her. It hardly loses credibility by being uttered by her father irrespective of any other act he may have committed. Clearly, upon realizing his request did not have a reasonable expectation of fulfillment, he chose to end his own life, taking very valuable secrets to the grave which might have provided some closure to people who are grieving and traumatized.

Psycholegally, despite the premeditation, we can look at Samantha Koenig and the Couriers not only in isolation but against the background of the other murders Keyes is suspected to have committed. Freud spoke of the instinct for self-destruction, could that not be even more acute in psychopaths? The import lies in whether we interpret Israel Keyes as legally insane or not. Since Keyes killed himself before he could be tried, which constitutes a significant failure of our carceral system, his example cannot be used as legal precedent. Speculatively, there is an unexplored argument that despite displaying the trappings of rationality, Keyes was in fact enslaved by an insanity that rose up from deep within his subconscious. That possession by chthonic forces led to the destruction of currently innumerable lives, as well as his own. Maybe his daughter's too. His expectation that all of that could be assuaged by a speedy execution indicates a significant lack of understanding. Israel Keyes may not have been the best person to defend himself. In our adversarial system, justice is only ever properly served in the face of a good defense. Still, confessions do not hurt either.

Categorical dismissal of the possibility of remorse in such extreme cases poorly serves investigators, the public and the interests of justice. It is well established that feelings of guilt tend to result in increased compliance. Duly expressed remorse can effect such issues as sentencing, rehabilitation and parole, even though it seems to have a negligible ability to inspire forgiveness in the aggrieved. In the case of violent offenses, it has been shown that responses lean heavily towards believing such expressions are insincere. Although without question malingering exists, its detection is extraordinarily difficult, and even the most advanced methods have significant limitations. In the absence of reliable science and questionable "gut" instincts remorse may exist more as potential tool than some sort of spiritual or ethical aspiration. Sincere or not, rejection of such expressions leads towards resentment, as inevitably does punishment as well, which is unlikely to increase legal compliance. Whether or not punitive measures are truly an imperative part of the sanctions against offenders can be questioned altogether. Retribution is as old as time itself, and indeed the law exists in part to satisfy the perceived need for personal vengeance. Humanity currently exists at a scale and scientific acumen never before achieved. Methodologies that would be familiar to Cro-Magnon man and are questionably effective based on empirical evidence hardly speaks well to our cultural advancement.

Morality and ethics do not necessarily exist in the light of empirical evidence, but often enough in spite of their absence. Freud stated that the legal prohibition against killing, and the consequences that ensue from the violation of the prohibition, is in part to assuage the jealousy of those who might wish to act similarly. Perhaps part of the origin of our cultural fascination with the psychopath is our envy of their fearlessness. Collectively we have chosen an almost tyrannical collegiality, which if sometimes forced, is thought better than the chaos that might result from lawlessness. We have chosen this, which means we could choose to do it differently. Sometimes we do, though the consequences are rarely as liberating as we might have hoped.

Justice could be said to serve three functions: punishment of the guilty, sequestration of the dangerous and the rehabilitation of souls. I use the term "soul" in the nautical tradition, which continues to be used by airline pilots, to emphasize the importance of human life (as well as to distinguish them from corpses which were often aboard ships). What is a prison if not a ship that moves through time? Even as it remains spatially immobile those aboard cannot leave. It is an innate human trait to hold someone accountable when something terrible happens, and a necessary deterrent against irresponsible behavior. How we act when we do hold someone accountable is no less important, and arguably more, than the actions of the perpetrator. As Hemingway said, "being against evil doesn't make you good." Civilization is an extraordinarily fragile construct, subject to the whims of capricious Acts of God, no less so of men, and perhaps that is why intellectual deconstructionism is so threatening. It is far more comfortable to reside in binary answers such as right and wrong, but progress is often uncomfortable, and subject to discontinuity.

In any system that can be exploited by bad actors, bad actors will exploit it. Particularly if not sufficiently deterred. Any human system of sufficient scale will have injustice as a non-zero phenomenon. We all face moral hazard, and by and large, we all fail at least occasionally. The recognition of these universal, inevitable failures as such is imperative to human survival. Dealing with the consequences of our flawed humanity should not be viewed merely as, or even best served by, the rejection of aberrance but rather the expected and worthy task of all sentient beings. Lao Tzu states in the Tao Te Ching that "a bad man is a good man's job." The recognition of the inescapability from injustice should lead us to be more vigilant, not more fatalistic and resigned to our lot.

At the event horizon of a crime, two paths diverge. One is the perceived need of victims and co-victims to achieve retribution, because if you cannot or do not it is difficult to think of it as justice. On the other path is the rehabilitation of souls, because if you cannot or do not then you are not reducing the future injustices that will inevitably occur at their hands, which can happen as easily in prison as outside of it, if not more so. Without both the problem is unresolved. There could be few good reasons for the courts to categorically reject that a human soul is infinitely rehabilitable. "Anyone who fights with monsters should take care that he does not in the process become a monster," Nietzche warned. Certainly many people do see our government as a bit of a monster and given the scale and reach of it they can hardly be blamed.

The individual is already given special provenance by the United States, since our founders feared exactly such a scenario, as codified not only by our liberty being considered as having transcendent value, but the recognition that imprisonment does not abrogate all human rights. Even in the absence of cosmic comment, if our existence is considered strictly bounded by the biological determinants of birth and death, people are "endowed by their creator with certain inalienable rights" and deserve the consideration of potentially remedial opportunities even on the remotest chance of their success. Many spiritual traditions assert that forgiveness is more potent than vengeance, and we often claim to believe it. We rarely act like we do.

The government does exist in part to monopolize violence and punishment. Though hardly an ideal solution, it is superior to a hobbesian war of all against all. Again, injustices are the expected outcome of any large organizational system. Theoretically, there is no legal condition which may not be changed by a single instance of injustice, and this is a very good standard to have, and the very premise of law based on precedent. Our legal system presupposes that not everything relevant to jurisprudence has been written down yet. The record of the law is seen as an infinitely improvable document. Although it is designed not to regress in its understanding, it does assume a just world hypothesis in which human systems are of penultimate importance short of a divine prerogative on which it makes no comment. As the US system has no tradition of the divine right of kings, and indeed formed in opposition to all claims of individual sovereignty by any actor and did so against the vastest empire the planet has ever seen, no legal status quo is permanently unassailable.

Psycholegal questions can suffer from a prejudice of recency while hypocritically adhering to a standard of mental competency determined over a century ago. Some distinction should be made between the incorrigible criminal and the otherwise aspiring productive citizen who has acted in error. We can see evidence of this in even the worst offenders if we look hard enough. Loss of liberty is the punishment and may be continued indefinitely in some cases without oppressively high security incarceration amongst the most predatory of the imprisoned. Those showing promise of rehabilitation, any promise at all, can be housed in strictly supervised environments that are nonetheless not specifically designed to be punitive.

An increased perception of fairness and mercy that is nonetheless retributive could increase legal compliance and cooperation in the community. As examples increase, others will inevitably follow suit (Roy, 2021, p. 239). Rather than a system that feeds resentments in a feedback loop, the very act of regulating liberty as gently as possible could increase the perceived credibility of the criminal justice system. Existence is a potentially improvable condition, but likely only with the maximum participation by all stakeholders, which includes not only greater compliance with the law, but fairer laws to comply with.

"THIS HAS TO HAPPEN"

On February 7, 2022 Isaac Eames killed his 21-year-old son Troy, his dog and attempted to kill his wife Karen by shooting her in the face twice before turning the gun on himself and dying from a bullet that entered his brain. Eames was a Sheriff's Deputy in the Onondaga Sheriff's department where he was specifically and solely in charge of numerous accounts used by the department for various reasons and also wrote grant proposals for the department. Deputy Eames allegedly colluded with his wife to embezzle over half a million dollars in the last few years, largely to fund an expensive lifestyle he could not otherwise afford. His activity had been flagged by the bank, and he had come under investigation.

Deputy Eames may have committed these offences, both embezzlement and murder, due to strain. General strain theory assumes crime occurs when individuals are unable to cope with accumulated strains in a positive, legal, and socially constructive manner." Association with deviant peer can predict the occurrence of crime while under strain, which begs the general question about the atmosphere at the Onondaga Sherrif's department. The behavior of other deputies was brought into question by the press after they seemed responsible for unnecessarily escalating a minor conflict at a high school football game where they were providing security. Eames may have felt entitled to a more affluent lifestyle than he could legally afford. It is possible that issues in the Sheriff's department went beyond his own activities, or more likely a permissive culture existed that allowed for the flaunting of rules and standards. It is quite a leap from simple police misconduct, or even extensive embezzlement, to family annihilation. While the rest of the department certainly cannot be held accountable for Eames actions, small inflections from normative behavior early on can lead to radical departures the further one goes from the origin point.

Deputy Eames may have killed son Troy to spare him the embarrassment of being labeled as the son of a criminal, or perhaps he had knowingly participated in his father's criminality and could implicate others. For some reason which is unclear from press reports, Eames spared his daughter. Within interactionist theories, deviance is understood as emerging from the interactions and interpretations within a particular social situation. In other words, even if Troy had not been complicit in his father's embezzlement scheme, his murder may have been a pseudo-altruistic act of his father protecting him from the consequences of the allegations that were about to come out. However, Troy was not a child. His obituary describes him as a "big kid", and indeed at 21 years of age he is fully in his majority. His photograph shows a robust and bearded young man. Whether or not Troy may have knowingly participated in his parent's illegal activity, beyond merely going on vacation with them, is unknown but it may be merely parsimonious to see his murder as the elimination of a threat of some kind, to some goal Deputy Eames may have had for after his death. Exactly how a father uses rationalization, as is proposed by the neutralization theory of crime whereby people can rationalize even the most horrific acts, is very difficult to parse conclusively. Neutralization theory argues that many criminals, despite their actions, still desire to be seen as good people and maintain connections to conventional society. To reconcile their criminal behavior with their self-image as good people, neutralization theory suggests that criminals use various techniques to ease their conscience before or after committing the crime.

Deputy Eames feelings of relative deprivation, and a narcissistic contempt for his colleagues, justified a maladaptive grandiosity. He may have given short shrift to the idea that he would be caught embezzling, or perhaps he premeditated his family annihilation with a fearlessness sometimes seen in frontal lobe disorders. The extent to which Deputy Eames family may have been in thrall to him is unclear, but certainly the embezzlement would not have been possible without him and his particular position at the Onondaga County Sheriff's Department. It seems reasonable to speculate that others in the department may also have benefited from his activities, perhaps in ways much better hidden than Eames's own crimes were.

Deputy Eames has a surviving daughter. Her whereabouts during the murders has not been released to the press and only brief mention is made of her in Troy's obituary. If we speculate Troy was murdered in a pseudo-altruistic act of protection, we must question why he shot the dog. Dogs are sometimes killed or otherwise neutralized in order to prevent discovery of a crime which can be facilitated by their barking. Again, he may have considered it an altruistic act as after the family was destroyed, there would be no one to take care of the dog. We may even reasonably expect that the dog would have been quite traumatized by events and Eames saw that as a mercy killing as well. His wife's survival and escape was unanticipated. If Karen and Troy were both complicit in his crimes, and he perceived a larger conspiratorial threat against his daughter possibly from other corrupt elements, it could have facilitated his rationalization of the murder of his family. Apparently before he began shooting Deputy Eames merely said, "this has to happen." Exactly why he thought so is something the rest of us can only wonder about, as we can never know.

TRAUMA

Post Traumatic Stress Disorder (PTSD) is defined in the DSM-5 as a persistent and disabling condition in response to some traumatic event which the sufferer has experienced, which can include harm or death to a loved one, whether witnessed or unwitnessed. Stimuli reminiscent of the event can create intrusive thoughts, vivid memories surrounding the event and at the extreme, dissociative events where it feels as if the traumatic event is recurring. These thoughts may even follow the victim into their sleep in the form of distressing dreams, which can result in sleep disturbance or the avoidance of sleep altogether. The difficulty in processing the trauma can lead to extended periods of feeling that waking life has more dream-like qualities and a disturbing sense of unreality. Withdrawal, anhedonia, generalized negativity, exaggerated startle response, irritability, hypervigilance and even amnesia can all be symptoms of PTSD. A person with PTSD may attempt to avoid any and all stimulation associated with the event and largely withdraw into their own dark world. In a terrible irony, people traumatized this way become more likely to commit acts of violence themselves,

It has been estimated every homicide costs between $15-$25 million, and the distinct nature of homicide as an act of malevolent intent gives it a distinct standing not only morally and societally, but in its ability to traumatize all involved. Homicide survivors can be considered co-victims of the event and may experience symptoms of PTSD for up to five years after the loss of their loved one. These symptoms for this length of time for this very specific population are all but inevitable. In addition to the immediate co-victims of a murder, this trauma extends to multiple degrees of separation and can easily embroil an entire community with possible contagion to national and even international levels. Often the killers themselves are the first people traumatized by their own act and may never recover from what they have done to regain normal functioning. Although the DSM-5 insists the traumatic connection cannot occur through electronic media this could be viewed as an anachronistic caveat worthy of further review.

On a summer day in the late 90's in Jasper, Texas a Black man named James Byrd Junior was gruesomely murdered after being lured into a truck by three White men in a brutal hate crime. Beaten into submission, he was tied up and dragged behind the truck for several miles. It is believed he remained conscious through the ordeal until his body was slammed into a curb as the truck turned a corner, decapitating him. The horrific act and the outpouring of grief and outrage, both within the town and far beyond, shattered the community's sense of security and left them bound together by a deep collective wound. Media attention from around the world engulfed the entire community as global attention was brought to the problem of racism in the American South. Not only was the community shocked by the horrific details of James Byrd Junior's death, but being labeled as a terrible small town compounded the injury with insult. People were ashamed they were from Jasper. It is beyond good fortune that in contrast to these unspeakable acts, the high character of many within the town is beyond doubt, and the wisdom they deployed in response to the scrutiny is impossible to second guess. Particularly James Byrd Jr.'s surviving family was a voice of peace and reconciliation, a heavy burden to bear in addition to their grief. Nonetheless, years out the violent crime rate and divorce had both substantially increased, likely as a trauma response. While Jasper's story is ultimately one of resilience, it also suggests a need to explore the role of social capital in such journeys. A deeper understanding of these networks could be key. As relates to the avoidance behavior associated with PTSD, the entire town of Japser, and even larger cognitive objects like "Texas", "The South" and "America" can be troubling mnemonics. The dark archetype of The Good Ol' Boy had reared its ungodly head and terrified the world.

PTSD may be as likely to develop from having known someone who was murdered as from having seen someone get murdered whether you knew them or not. The mind's eye and perseveration provide the requisite horror. In mass murder events, where a significant amount of territory is considered unsafe by the co-victims, and a necessarily authoritative police response is required, some people whose closest exposure to the event was hearing sirens developed PTSD and could be retraumatized just by hearing them again. Simply not knowing the status of a loved one or even close friend during such an event can be enough to trigger multiple symptoms of the disorder for an extended period even if the person in question is found safe. Murder is to trauma what plutonium is to radiation: it doesn't take much.

Murder anniversaries can be a delicate time for co-victims. The legal system can compound this effect by its deliberative pacing and sometimes perceived indifference. Some training of court officers and reform of the judicial process itself which allows victims to put their own statements on the record has begun an overdue reconciliation process between law enforcement and the populations they serve, but much work remains to be done. Particularly in economically disadvantaged populations, where many murders occur, the perception that law enforcement is indifferent or even vaguely complicit lessens the available resources to which the development of PTSD is proportionally related in any conceivable traumatic event, but as cannot be emphasized enough, particularly with homicide. Most of the public has no idea who they are supposed to contact if they are struggling as a co-victim of a murder. The applications for various public assistance programs can be nebulous, excessively bureaucratic and stingy. And if justice is meant to be swift, public assistance is not. Murder shatters families, just as often of the murderer's as anyone else's. People may take sides in grudges and outright feuds that can last for generations. Most murders occur between individuals in the same community. People who often know each other well. The wreckage of a single murder can stain a geography for an indeterminate length of time. Looking for enantiodromian positive outcomes in the wake of a murder is a daunting and depressing task, bearing its own frisson of trauma.

The failure rate for explaining the human mind is one hundred percent. Murder co-victims are often filled with thoughts of revenge, and it is impossible not to empathize with them. Perhaps just as interesting a question as 'why do so many people murder?' is 'why do so many people do not murder?' Human aggression evolved with us because it so often turned out to be advantageous, even necessary. In ancient societies murder was more a less a civil matter, in more feudal times the society of orders cared much more about *who* you murdered than *why* you did and counted themselves as among the most civilized of men. Ostensibly in the United States all citizens have equal protection under the law. In practice it is more complicated than that.

In light of the tremendous cost of murder, both financially and in more humanitarian views, significant resources towards the prevention of its occurrence and the mitigation of its effects is more than justified, it is imperative and overdue. Models, which are always wrong but occasionally useful, of a collective response must be examined, analyzed and likely amended with great frequency. Sociogenic trauma resulting from homicide should be counteracted when at all possible. Behavioral therapy and other interventions from the standard medical model of psychiatry show some efficacy, but making sense after a homicide is uniquely challenging. Much more study is required, followed close on pertinent legislation and the allocation of resources. All three span the full range from inadequate to nonexistent. Indeed, hostility to the very idea is widespread. The studies that exist have significant limitations, not least of all their small sample size and the self-selection of participants. Those suffering the most with PTSD as a result of being proximate to homicide would likely avoid further reminders, such as participating in a study, making the results at hand difficult to generalize. The problem is embarrassingly common in the United States and by definition is a public health crisis. A crisis largely ignored outside of sensationalist news reports which themselves add to the trauma.

TERROR IN THE STREETS

Public awareness, as well as efforts by legislators and law enforcement, has yet to be reflected in scholarship on how best to thwart the rise in mass shootings, or even certainty that such a rise exists. Even what constitutes a mass shooting is contentious. Depending on the parameters of the study, many mass shootings are not included in various studies. True terrorist attacks and school shootings are comparatively rare in a field that might be best described as *rampage violence*. Beyond definitions, and important subsets of rampage violence, any attempt to reduce the number of mass shootings or even the casualties that result from them are hindered by the inability to increase the power of gun control laws, the generalized secrecy with which such plots are hatched and the very nature of mass shootings themselves where lethality is cataclysmically sudden. Perhaps the best way to foil mass shooting plots is from the mass shooters themselves, begging the question as to whether at least some portion of mass shooters want to be stopped. According to the FBI's assessment, a significant portion of active shooters directly communicate their intent to harm a target or disclose plans to a third party, providing clues about potential mass shootings. Most incidents were demonstrably preventable based on information known about the offenders beforehand. Not all rampage violence is treated equally by the press however, high body counts tend to get the most attention, while foiled plots may not even make the news. Certainly not the headlines. Forensic psychologists depend on these media reports in order to better understand the phenomenon and may not be best served by the capitalist media paradigm of "if it bleeds, it leads." Those plots that are foiled are most often foiled because of leakage, but even in those cases where such leakage is reported to law enforcement prevention is not universal as was clearly evidenced by the shameful performance of law enforcement and medical personnel in the mass shooting in Lewiston, Maine where Robert Card killed 18 people on October 25, 2023. Numerous warnings were made, and numerous opportunities to stop him were missed. The type of mass shooter most likely to be stopped is usually seeking to gain fame from his intended act, and cannot seem to help themselves but to tell people their intentions.

There are significant questions as to whether the United States is an outlier in mass shootings or merely mass shootings of a specific stripe. While mass shootings occur globally, lone-wolf attacks are a less frequent phenomenon outside of the US. Perhaps part of the horror of American mass shootings is the idea that an isolated person could hatch a plot of such extreme lethality. However, mass casualty events are not unknown in the rest of the world, though they are more commonly perpetrated by what could be called *packs of wolves.* The United States, characterized by high ethnic diversity and a focus on personal autonomy, stands out from cultures with stronger kinship ties and a more collective identity. In other words, mass shootings in America are less of a societally unique phenomenon than they are a uniquely American expression of one of humanity's worst tendencies. One commonly used definition of a mass shooting come from an NYPD report, which requires the following elements be present: (a) involved a firearm, (b) appeared to have struck random strangers or bystanders and not only specific targets, and (c) not occurred solely in domestic settings or have been primarily gang-related, drive-by shootings, hostage-taking incidents, or robberies. It is worth noting this definition does not exclude terrorism.

The profoundly anti-social nature of mass shootings may simply be the ultimate expression of people who are anti-social more generally. Research reveals a disturbing link between mass shootings and prior acts of domestic violence or stalking, with a substantial number of perpetrators exhibiting such behavior. Ian David Long, who killed a dozen people and injured a dozen more in a bar he frequented in Thousand Oaks, California, paused his carnage to post on social media that his motivation was simple boredom, but he had a history of presenting troubling behavior and was reportedly easily angered. While federal law bars abusers with misdemeanor domestic violence convictions from buying guns, loopholes and uneven state enforcement often allow them to keep existing firearms, putting victims at risk. Legislative paranoia about anything that could be perceived as taking people's guns gives law enforcement few tools in few places to keep the profoundly anti-social from being armed well enough to commit atrocities. Violence, like charity, often begins at home. Deep fractures within the home can exacerbate existing social tensions, potentially leading to violent outbursts. In this way, domestic dysfunction can be seen as a root cause of some mass violence incidents. It could also be argued that cases where violence of any stripe is perpetrated in the public sphere it is unlikely to be absent from the home. Whether this connection justifies more stringent control of gun access and ownership to those convicted or charged with domestic violence promises to be a contentious debate, should such a debate ever occur (Note: I wrote this some time before the *US v Rahimi* went before the Supreme Court where Justice Thomas's absolutely brain dead originalism argument for gun control was tested, and where he remained the sole dissenting voice. I decided to keep the original). One could imagine that the part of the Second Amendment which mentions "a well regulated militia" might hold equal weight with "the right to keep and bear arms". Very little about guns seems terribly well regulated.

Lack of understanding about mass shooters can lead us to project our own unresolved issues onto them. This creates an 'us vs. them' mentality, where we distance ourselves from the problem and look for external blame, hindering efforts to address the root causes. By thinking of mass shootings as incomprehensible tragedies or relegating them to war oriented thinking by labeling them terrorism, we miss potential opportunities to thwart them more often. The etymology of the word gun is derived from the Scandinavian Gunhildr, which means "battle-maiden". Gunhildr was a quasi-historical figure known for her cruelty and violence. Some theoretical frameworks within criminal psychology posit a connection between mass shootings and a distorted sense of empowerment which can even be interpreted as perversely erotic in its nature. This could manifest as a symbolic phallus representing control or dominance, particularly for perpetrators experiencing feelings of profound powerlessness or emasculation. The gun, for some, symbolizes the ability to resist oppression and defend what they believe is right. The gun functions as a talisman, offering a sense of security and control.

Journalists, as well as the American people, as well as the shooters themselves have come to view coverage of rampage killings as tragically routine; the predictability also results in contagion and encourages fame-seeking by the perpetrators of this most public form of violence. Reporting on mass shootings presents a complex ethical landscape. Journalists must balance informing the public with respecting the victims and avoiding glorifying the perpetrators. Nonetheless, journalists still strongly favor releasing the shooter's name and photograph, lean towards sharing statements by shooter and deny they are encouraging a contagion effect. However, the strength of these opinions varies widely depending on the specific job in the media they are tasked with, as well as previous experience covering mass shootings.

Mass shootings disproportionately target minority populations and show a positive connection to Violent Political Rhetoric (VPR) in the public sphere. VPR is bipartisan and has a long history in the US and indeed internationally. VPR manifests in a spectrum of severity. Key components include the intensity of hatred expressed, the presence of implicit or explicit calls to violence, attacks on human dignity, and the targeting of specific groups or individuals, often through scapegoating. If the intent of VPR is to encourage those susceptible to its messages to engage in actions they might not otherwise consider, or at least would not consider in the absence of the justification provided by their darkest thoughts being seemingly aired out in the marketplace of ideas, then VPR is an extremely effective mechanism. In all likelihood, the purveyors of VPR have as their intent the simple rallying of a polity to become more politically engaged (ie attend rallies, donate money, vote etc.) it is now undeniable that certain outliers in any group can be incited to turn metaphor into more solid action. There is a degree to which mass shootings can be interpreted as very much a crisis manufactured by those political operatives with little regard for human life and public safety.

Contagion exists not only to possibly increase the number of mass shootings, but in-depth coverage provides would be shooters with the opportunity to more effectively plan and execute their plots. A critical question surrounding the phenomenon of mass shootings is the potential for contagion. The possibility that media coverage or details of one mass shooting event can inspire or influence future attacks is a very real concern. Researchers are exploring the nature of this potential link, investigating whether exposure to such events can trigger copycat killings or desensitize individuals already at risk. Mathematics commonly used in seismology to understand earthquakes and their aftershocks, have been used to approach the periodicity of mass shootings. By employing more sophisticated statistical models, we can calculate the likelihood that a specific mass shooting was triggered by a prior event, as opposed to being an isolated incident unrelated to contagion. Most analyzed data sets categorize a significant portion of mass shootings as potentially influenced by prior events. However, a substantial number are still considered isolated incidents.

When mass shootings occur, it is common and quite understandable that the press and the public speculate on the mental health of the perpetrator. However, psychosis plays a role in mass shootings in only a minority of cases. This not only adds to the stigma already suffered by the mentally ill but ignores the fact that less than 5% of all crimes are committed by the mentally ill. In particular mass shooters are often described as psychotic to the degree that it has become so a part of colloquial parlance as to lose much of its diagnostic value in such discussions. Psychosis, characterized by fixed false beliefs (delusions), sensory experiences not based on reality (hallucinations), and disturbed thinking patterns, is a significant condition. However, pinpointing the exact role psychosis plays in a specific event is crucial, as it's not simply a matter of semantics. A critical aspect of understanding mass shootings involves examining the perpetrator's mental state at the time of planning and execution. This analysis should focus on the severity and nature of any symptoms they were experiencing, and how these symptoms might have influenced their decision-making. This task is complicated by the fact that nearly 60% of mass shooters die at the scene, often within minutes, thus making it impossible to examine their motivations *ex post facto*. Although a quarter of mass shooters had some history of psychosis, which is well above the background rate, roughly 60% of perpetrators had some mental health history, meaning any interaction with the mental health system, which is only slightly higher than the general population. In the vast majority of cases, psychosis played absolutely no role in the commission of the crime. In only 10% of cases psychosis was the major motivating factor, and it is roughly equally split among the remaining 20% of cases as to whether psychosis played a minor or moderate role in the act.

Could America's well-known problem with inequality be contributing to a rise in mass shootings? At first glance they are historically coincident. The relative deprivation of income inequality should be distinguished from the absolute deprivation of poverty, although both are correlated with negative outcomes particularly in the field of public health which mass shootings can be categorized as. Some theories suggest a correlation between significant income inequality within communities and higher levels of social unrest, such as anger, frustration, resentment, and violence. Mass shootings, indiscriminate killings, do not seem related to absolute poverty at all. However, areas with high income inequality or relative deprivation may create a breeding ground for social discontent, potentially fostering a sense of frustration and resentment that some studies have shown to correlate with mass shootings. Although most places will never experience a mass shooting at all, those with higher income inequality seem more prone to them to a degree which is statistically significant.

Machine learning and AI may offer some hope of predicting and preventing mass shooting. A growing body of research explores the link between social conditions and mass shootings, investigating how factors like poverty, inequality, and social isolation might contribute to these tragedies. The majority of perpetrators were shown to have both a mood disorder and a stressor surrounding their employment. While such modeling using machine learning is only in its infancy, as is the entire field of AI, it does hold some promise of future understandings which will allow for possible early warnings and intervention measures. Perhaps some day we will fully understand all the complexities that go in to these horrors, and be able to get out in front of them before they happen, but that day is not here yet.

AFTERWORD

It is very important to remember that crime is going *down*. You would not believe that from watching the news, which is why most people don't. Some of you who just read that sentence do not believe me, but it nonetheless has the benefit of being true. Exactly why it is going down is no less of a mystery than why it happens to begins with, and just as worthy of exploration. Having said that, it is no excuse to drop the ball, but rather should refocus our efforts. Currently I weigh about 180 pounds, and I could still stand to lose a pound or two. My fighting weight is around 165. When I was 30 years old I ruptured a disc in my back, causing me severe sciatica for many years. I also got divorced around the same time. Just a wonderful time in my life. When I got out of bed at all it was usually just to stuff myself with terrible delivery pizza and drink as many beers as I had managed to limp home from the store with. One of the few real pleasures I had in life was eating sweets, which I often did until it just about made me sick. Unsurprisingly, I shot up to 250 pounds, which I carried terribly. I had a gigantic gut, skinny legs and no ass. Eventually I finally got serious about trying to lose the weight, which is absolutely one of the hardest things I have ever had to do. At some point, the moment itself does not remain in memory, I realized I had lost 35 pounds. All I can really tell you is that I still did not look or feel like it was time to take a victory lap (swimming was easier on my sciatica anyway). In fact, I was only halfway to where I am now, and twenty years later it is not getting any easier to keep the weight off. My point is that that is where America is now with crime, murder in particular. For decades, despite all that is truly great and truly exceptional about this country, we were the shame of the Western World when it comes to crime. Our murder rates have been 5-10 times higher than any of our peers, and as their crime rates have also been dropping, we are still comparatively an outlier. Shamefully so in my opinion, but do not dare say I am unpatriotic. Those are fighting words where I come from.

My father's ashes are interred at Arlington National Cemetery. A former Marine who stood by a door in the White House during the Cuban Missile Crisis for hours on end in case a Kennedy might want to walk through it, after a successful business career he returned to government to become a founding member of the Department of Homeland Security. In his 60's he worked 12 hour days, six days a week in the face of Katrina. After 9/11 he worked on teams trying to figure out how random bits of flesh smeared on chunks of concrete could be identified and catalogued so that families could get their loved one's remains. *All* of their remains. He did things at Mount Weather he couldn't talk to me about at all, since officially Mount Weather does not exist. One thing he did tell me, which I am sure he wasn't supposed to, was that deep below ground at Mount Weather, there is a cafeteria. Nothing exceptional except for the relatively high rate of pay the cafeteria workers made, since you need a top secret clearance to sling hash in this particular cafeteria. In order to get your free meal in this cafeteria you are supposed to bring a punch card. It's not a retinal eye scan or a hand print reader, just a simple piece of paper with set spots where the lunch lady uses a hole punch to mark that you had your free meal that day. I am not sure if this was meant to curtail unnecessary government spending or something, but that's how it works. My father, a much smarter man than me in many ways (although I've got some game), was roughly equally as forgetful without having had the excuse of being stoned for his 20's. One day, he forgot his card. The lunch lady, who was as archetypal a lunch lady as can be imagined, seemed a touch annoyed but waived him through regardless telling him to bring it the next day. He forgot it the next day too, which for a moment I guess caused him a slight thrill of anxiety. He apologized profusely. As a young Marine who knows what horrible punishment might have ensued for such a breach of government protocol in a top secret facility.

"Honey," she said, putting a fist on her oversized hip, "this is Mount Weather. I know you ain't here for the meatloaf."

Despite the drop in crime, I am actually very afraid for America at the moment. The 2024 Presidential election campaign is in full swing, and without making partisan comment, it is certainly as ugly as any I have seen in my lifetime. A big part of our current debate is about distrust in our government, and not without some cause. But there are some things that only government can do. Responding to crime is chief among them. You cannot privatize your way to a lower crime rate. The private prison system has been a disaster and should be abolished. Our lack of a social safety net worthy of the name is doubtless a large part of why crime is so bad, and the key difference between us and our western peers. We are the richest country in the world. We also have the highest rate of childhood poverty, and that is only the beginning of a long list of things which are not going well here. It will not take much for the crime rate to spike again. Indeed, during the pandemic, that is exactly what happened, even with most people trapped at home. As was said in one of my essays, every murder that happens costs between $15-$25 million dollars. What are we willing to spend to try and keep that happening? If you want to know, the best person to ask is someone who has lost a loved one to such malevolence.

Punishment is not working. Shame is not working.

Incarceration is not working. In many cases all of these things are absolutely appropriate, but we cannot just end the discussion there. Personally, I don't think any of those things have much to do with the drop in crime. In any human system of sufficient scale injustice will always be a nonzero phenomenon. Taking an eye for an eye threatens to leave everyone blind. There will always be people unable or unwilling to handle the personal responsibility required by our increasingly complex world. Literally in the last decade humans are dealing with forces which simply have not existed for the previous quarter of a million years of our existence. Praise, empathy and support have been given short shrift so far, and might be worth a try, sometimes even in the most extreme cases. We will not know when to do what until we better understand why these things happen, and right now we are not working very hard to do that. So I am doing my best to do my part, and if it seems like progressive psychobabble to you, I can only say that sometimes it seems that way to me too. I am doing my best to understand, and to contribute, in the vague hope that somewhere, maybe, my father will be proud of me and know that I am trying to carry on his legacy..

I miss you dad.

www.ingramcontent.com/pod-product-compliance
Lightning Source LLC
Chambersburg PA
CBHW071835210526
45479CB00001B/142